TOP TIPS FOR VISITING THE TOKYO DISNEY RESORT

Kevin Yee

Ultimate Orlando Press
Orlando, Florida

Top Tips for Visiting the Tokyo Disney Resort
by Kevin Yee

2016 EDITION
Printed in the United States of America

To Devon and Tyler

Like most long projects, this book was written with the generous support and help of others. Without them, the experience on these pages would be much poorer. I owe each of these individuals a debt of gratitude for their kind assistance:

- **Taduyuki Hara**, for an initial head start in research.
- **"TDLFan," Richard Kaufman, Dave and Hiroko Haskell, "Joe in Tokyo," Michael Snyder, Ted Tamburo, Felix Cooper, "SuperDry," Tim Kurkoski, Jason Punk, and Mark Schrimsher,** for proofreading, fact-checking, and lending me their jaw-dropping expertise about the Tokyo Disney Resort.
- **Patricia Hirane**, for assisting me with updated menu and price information.
- **Steve Bauer**, for his customary eagle eye in line-editing and polishing.

Foreword

Visiting a foreign country can be daunting. This is especially true if you don't speak the language. Things get really complicated when the signs around you are in characters you cannot decipher or even begin to sound out. Apart from language issues, there are little cultural differences that keep life interesting. You may know to take off your shoes when entering a home. Would you have known to bus your own table at a food court, or to avoid blowing your nose in public? English-speaking visitors face a tough dilemma: they either fret at every turn about the right things to do, adding stress to the trip; or else they vow not to worry so much, and they risk looking like uninformed tourists uninterested in local customs and uncaring about the right things to do.

There's a third way. Becoming informed about the necessities removes any uncertainty. This book was designed to keep your vacation as stress-free as possible, avoiding not only the big problems that ruin trips, but also the small ones that chip away at the magic. With this book, you'll know how to "do as the Romans do" on your vacation.

You'll also find information about every step of your journey, from arriving at the airport, transferring to the hotel, and making your way to the theme parks, to what to expect when you buy food or gifts. Because this book focuses so specifically on the journey to the Tokyo Disney Resort, you'll find the exact information you need, rather than vague generalities.

Visitors with more time and an adventurous bent may desire to explore more of Tokyo and Japan, and this book will offer tips to make that easier, too.

Table of Contents

Planning the Trip

More than any other strategy, tip, or trick, the one thing that will impact your vacation the most is the advance planning, especially the timing. There are numerous variables in play, and if all of them align properly, things will proceed with maximum smoothness. Otherwise, you may be facing larger crowds, higher hotel prices, or difficult commuter conditions.

Timeline

More information about each of these topics can be found in the sections below. This section serves only to get you thinking about deadlines for the most important topics.

One of the first things you should do when considering a trip to Tokyo is to obtain a passport. This can be accomplished in as little as twelve weeks, but why cut things close? Aim instead for six months. Post offices can issue passports, but you may find smaller lines at a county clerk's office. You won't need a visa to visit Japan for a short vacation lasting less than three months. For longer visits, it's best to enquire to be sure.

If you're planning on staying at a Disney hotel, you'll want to make those reservations several months in advance too— reservations may be made up to six months early. It is especially important to reserve rooms in advance if your destination is the MiraCosta Hotel, since it is in such high demand.

For non-Disney hotels near the Resort and other hotels around Japan, make reservations 3-6 months out, using an agent that specializes in this sort of thing, such as Rakuten Travel (http://travel.rakuten.co.jp/en).

Flights are actually cheapest if you wait until 2-3 months before your vacation, since discount travel agency I-ACE (http://www.iace-usa.com – click on the "English" button) does not list flights until the three-month point. It's safe to wait this long, but if waiting makes you uncomfortable, you can always try Orbitz (www.orbitz.com) or Travelocity (www.travelocity.com) to book a flight further in advance.

One to two months before you travel, arrange for a Japan Rail Pass (if you plan to buy one). This must be purchased before your vacation begins.

Deciding How Many Days to Stay

How familiar are you with Disney parks already? How much of a Disney fanatic are you? The answers to these questions dictate how long you may wish to spend at Tokyo Disney parks. In general, you can see Tokyo Disneyland in 1-2 days and Tokyo DisneySea in 1-3 days. If you're unfamiliar with Disney parks, plan to spend two days in each park. If you're highly familiar with Disney parks but consider yourself a

major fan, you may want to spend two days in each park. Tokyo DisneySea is a park unlike any other Disney park in the world. It will possibly capture your imagination more than Tokyo Disneyland, but then again, there are many more rides in Tokyo Disneyland than in Tokyo DisneySea.

If you already know other Disney parks well and consider yourself only a casual fan, you might only need one day to enjoy each park. This option may not provide enough time to experience every ride, particularly during busy seasons, but some of the rides are similar enough to American parks that this may not be a huge problem for casual fans.

When planning your trip, remember that multi-day park passports have to be used on consecutive days. This matters if you plan to spend some time off Disney property, exploring the city of Tokyo or other areas of the country. Be sure to lump your park visits together into one continuous block of days.

Choosing the Right Season

Japan is a country with four mostly mild seasons. Here's what you can expect in terms of climate:

Average Temperatures

December - March:
Lows of 34-40 degrees Fahrenheit (1-4° C)
Highs of 49-54 degrees Fahrenheit (9-12° C)
April - June:
Lows of 50-68 degrees Fahrenheit (10-20° C)
Highs of 65-77 degrees Fahrenheit (18-25° C)
July - September:
Lows of 68-76 degrees Fahrenheit (20-24° C)
Highs of 81-88 degrees Fahrenheit (27-31° C)
October - November:
Lows of 49-58 degrees Fahrenheit (9-14° C)
Highs of 61-70 degrees Fahrenheit (16-21° C)

Naturally, there will be day-to-day variations that differ significantly from these averages. But it's not just temperatures to consider. June and July constitute the rainy season, and the typhoon season stretches from August to October. In general, it rains a lot in Japan anyway, even in months that are not part of the usual rainy season. The month with the most rain, and the lightest crowds, is June.

July and August feature significant humidity in addition to the heat. You may also see humidity as late as September. The perceived temperature will be much higher on days with humidity; though the thermometer may indicate only 85 degrees, it will feel about 95 degrees if the humidity is oppressive.

It may surprise American travelers used to Disney parks (or ubiquitous highly air-conditioned venues in general) that not every building in the Tokyo Disney Resort is chilled to provide palpable respite from the weather outside. Temperatures are instead calibrated to be comfortable indoors, but not to impart instant cooling to those stepping inside. Some buildings and rides may, in fact, not feel air-conditioned at all, particularly during the "in-between" months when it's no longer summer, but winter still lies ahead, and the heater can be left turned off.

As you might expect from looking at these numbers, the ideal months to visit are April, May, October, and November. While October and November may be great in terms of milder temperatures and lessened humidity, there is still the minor threat of typhoons. Seasonal events like Halloween and Christmas also bring enhanced crowds to the parks. April and May therefore look to be more promising as a vacation period, but you will want to be careful that you don't overlap with Japanese school vacations. The school year ends in March, sending hordes of children and their families out into the countryside and major destinations. The next school year starts in April, so late April or early May might seem to be the ideal times to visit Japan. The Japanese have the same idea. They even have a name for it; "Golden Week" runs from the last couple of days in April until the first several days in May, and travelers from abroad are well-served to steer clear of the country during this hectic time. The weeks right before and after Golden Week, however, are much less crowded and often feature ideal weather.

Of course, March and April also bring the famous cherry blossoms in Japan, so it becomes a question of priorities. Do you wish to see this natural spectacle so badly that you will brave additional crowds to do so? If not, opt for October/November, or consciously choose a colder month to visit, knowing that crowds will be sparser and that parks will be open shorter hours. If you are a fan of Tokyo Disneyland's marvelous Halloween festivities which are unequalled at any other Disney Park, then late September is an excellent time to visit. The crowds have not yet swollen to October levels, but you get all the advantages of the seasonal decorations, show, and parade (this is analogous to visiting a Disney park in the U.S. in the first two weeks of December to take in the Christmas decorations, yet avoid the crowds).

Visiting during the heat of summer should be one of your last choices for the sake of physical comfort. Of course, if your own schedule dictates this must be the timing of your trip, you can at least find comfort in knowing that the parks will be fully opened, with no attraction refurbishments, and they will have later operating hours than is true in winter (alas, you'll need every one of those hours, since the crowds will be correspondingly denser in summer). August, in particular, is a busy time, as this is summer vacation in Japan.

Avoiding Crowded Days of the Week

During school holidays, almost every day is a busy day at the parks. But when school is in session, weekends are considerably busier at the Tokyo Disney Resort than weekdays. The difference is so noticeable, it greatly affects your ability to visit all the attractions. It would take at least two weekend days to see all the offerings at one of the parks, but midweek, you might be able to ride everything in a single day at Tokyo DisneySea. It would take more than one day for Tokyo Disneyland.

A large part of the visitor base at Tokyo Disney Resort consists of students taking field trips from local schools and residents of the Tokyo suburbs making day-trips out to the park (especially young couples and single females arriving and departing the same day by train). The local residents, in particular, are more likely to visit on weekends.

Another big chunk of visitors comes from farther afield and stay not only the weekend, but perhaps also an extra day. The spillover effect from such travelers means that Mondays and Fridays are still somewhat more crowded than other weekdays, and you may see this reflected in the prices of hotel rooms on these days. In general, fluctuating prices of the hotel rooms are excellent barometer for judging which days are going to be busy.

One strategy might be to concentrate park visits on Tuesday through Thursday, adding Monday (or Friday) if a fourth day is needed. Even if flying on a weekend becomes necessary, perhaps making the flight more expensive than it would be

otherwise, this is a worthwhile strategy to pursue. The additional cost incurred is more than balanced by the smaller lines you'll encounter when visiting the parks midweek.

If you can pursue that strategy, don't waste your time shopping until the end of your trip. Reserve all purchases for Friday, when the attractions will be more crowded. Shop in the early or middle part of the day—never at the end of the day when stores are mobbed.

Avoiding Commuter Hassles

As its name implies, Tokyo Disney Resort is located within the city of Tokyo, so the urban environment translates to packed commuter trains at certain times of the day. The train serving the Tokyo Disney Resort is a regular commuter train, not just an express train for the parks. If you try to arrive at the wrong hour, you'll be impossibly packed into the train. Don't try this with suitcases and other luggage!

Going to the parks midweek, as previously suggested, thus becomes a more difficult proposition if you plan to stay in a hotel away from the resort and take the train every morning.

Moving your airport days to the weekends has an added advantage insofar as you won't encounter a lot of packed trains (if you're using trains to get to the airport).

The alternative to train travel, the shuttle bus, uses regular highways and is subject to traffic delays. But the bigger problem you may face is that the shuttle bus only runs at certain hours of the day. The last shuttle for the Tokyo Disney Resort departs Narita airport at 5:05 p.m. You may wish to make plane reservations so as not to arrive after 4:00 p.m. (This leaves time for clearing customs, which involves photographing and fingerprinting all visitors over 16 years old.)

Avoiding Attraction Refurbishments

Almost every attraction is closed for a week or more on an annual basis for cleaning, repairing, and repainting. Visitors from abroad desiring to see every last ride face an unpalatable choice. Either they come during crowded peak seasons (summer or Christmas break) when the rides will all be operating, or they avoid crowds by visiting during non-peak seasons, when they will surely find at least a few attractions undergoing refurbishment.

If you don't want to simply hope for the best, you'll want to research attraction refurbishments before your trip, which are posted on the official Tokyo Disney Resort website roughly six months in advance:
http://www.tokyodisneyresort.co.jp/en/schedule/stop/index.html

On balance, it's probably better to avoid the crowds and miss a ride or two, as opposed to having everything open but having to brave big crowds. Typically, no more than one "E-Ticket" ride will be closed at a time, so even if you miss out on something, you'll still have a great day.

Selecting the Right Hotel

Once you've got the right dates nailed down for your visit, it's time to decide on a hotel.

There are three Disney-owned hotels: The Tokyo Disneyland Hotel, the MiraCosta, and the Disney Ambassador. The Tokyo Disneyland Hotel sits right at the entrance to Tokyo Disneyland and enjoys an unbeatable location. It is within walking distance to both the theme park and the Japan Rail (JR) station. It also features suites decorated with Disney characters, though these cost more than other rooms.

Similarly, the MiraCosta sits in front of Tokyo DisneySea. More accurately, it sits atop the entrance to Tokyo DisneySea. This hotel is actually inside the theme park gates! There's also a private entrance into the park from the hotel. Its posh interior and tremendous location add up to an unsurprisingly expensive per-night room cost. The most in-demand rooms are those with a harbor view, but savvy visitors on a budget may want to look for a room with only a partial harbor view. Those rooms are the least expensive, but they still boast a decent view of the inside of the park.

The Disney Ambassador Hotel is the odd man out in the group, as it is situated a bit farther away from either of the theme parks. Located at the far end of the shopping zone called Ikspiari, the Disney Ambassador is smaller than you'd

imagine. It does not have the expansive grounds or facilities you might be familiar with from visiting other Disney hotels worldwide, and it feels a bit more like a customary urban hotel. This is true, to some extent, of the MiraCosta as well. The common areas are somewhat small, and while one can wander through them freely, the experience is over pretty quickly. The MiraCosta is, however, extraordinarily posh for a Disney hotel.

The rooms at all three of the Disney hotels reflect the limitations of space common to every hotel in Japan—they will be smaller than similar rooms at U.S. Disney hotels.

To find information about any of the Disney hotels, visit http://www.tokyodisneyresort.co.jp/en/index.html. There, you can easily look up price and availability. You'll see that the season, and even the exact day of the week, feature different costs per night for the same room. Also, different rooms have different views, and thus have different pricing schemes. This lends some complexity to the online pricing chart, but if you're cautious, you can sort through the options readily enough to find the room(s) and price(s) that are best for you.

The Disney hotels offer restaurants, including character dining, that might make them worthwhile choices for your stay. To Westerners, the Disney hotel rooms may have a Japanese feel to them, with features such as a deep soaking tub, and smaller twin beds, rather than a single king-sized bed.

Many people enjoy the fact that hotel common areas and Guest rooms are decorated with Mickey Mouse and Disney brands. There's a channel on television looping endless videos about the parks, lending a feeling of being surrounded by the magic even after you leave the park for the day.

However, this level of immersiveness comes at a premium cost. The Disney hotels cost more than comparable hotels in downtown Tokyo. They also cost more than other hotels right in the same area around Tokyo Disney Resort. Confusingly known as "official hotels" (the designation came about because they existed before the Disney-owned hotels were built), the following non-Disney facilities are run by outside vendors and sometimes cost only half as much as the Disney hotels.

Official Hotels
Tokyo Bay Maihama Hotel
Sunroute Plaza Hotel
Tokyo Bay Hotel Tokyu
Hilton Tokyo Bay
Hotel Okura Tokyo Bay
Sheraton Grande Tokyo Bay Hotel

These hotels don't feature Disney characters in their rooms or have special Disney shows on television, but the rooms are just as nice, and, in some cases, even more posh. Only the Hilton and Sheraton go out of their way to cater to Western visitors.

The Tokyo Disney Resort website includes information about the official hotels:
http://www.tokyodisneyresort.co.jp/en/index.html.

Surprisingly, the facilities and common areas at the official hotels are more extensive than at the regular Disney hotels. For instance, the Disney hotels lack coin-operated laundry service, but most official hotels offer it at a reasonable price. There are very large arcades and play zones at some of the official hotels, most notably at the Sheraton. Some have beauty salons and chapels. Most have shops that carry official Tokyo Disney Resort merchandise, as well as sundries and snacks.

Some international visitors opt to avoid the official hotels because they are uncertain whether these hotels offer the same convenience as the regular Disney hotels. In fact, the official hotels offer access to the parks that is just as convenient as the regular Disney hotels, and, in fact, are more convenient than the Disney Ambassador Hotel (which is some distance away from the monorail stop). The official hotels are clustered together at one end of the Tokyo Disney Resort and have their own monorail stop named Bayside Station.

All of the official hotels are serviced by shuttle buses that spend all day moving back and forth between the monorail stop and the hotels. These shuttles get quite crowded at the end of the night and are standing-room only, and parents with strollers will need to fold them.

While all of the official hotels are technically within walking distance of the monorail stop, only the Hilton, the Okura, and the Sheraton are, practically speaking, within easy walking distance, so I recommend one of them.

The Hilton has a Starbucks for those needing a caffeine fix. Its restaurants are more upscale and a bit pricier than the other nearby hotels. There is also a fairly comprehensive shopping

area, as well as large common areas. A few computers in public areas allow for Internet access, which can be purchased by the minute.

The Okura doubles as a convention hotel, so its clientele is a bit different. As a result, its public areas are much smaller, more austere, and fewer in number. Also, there is practically nothing specifically geared for kids.

The Sheraton offers the best range of activities for children, including themed rooms geared to families, a large arcade, and an expansive play area with an admission fee of several dollars per hour. It has everything the Hilton has, but at a slightly reduced cost, and thus seems to be the best choice overall.  Since the Sheraton is part of the Starwood hotel group, you can join the Starwood Preferred Guest program at no charge (do this before the trip, if possible), and you'll be upgraded to a nicer room on a floor with free Internet access and a lounge with free drinks and snacks. If being surrounded by Disney magic 24 hours a day is important, stay at a regular Disney hotel. Otherwise, the Sheraton offers the best value and should be your first choice.

There's one final category of hotels: those further away from the Resort but still in the Shin-Urayasu region, and thus quite close. This category bears an equally confusing moniker: they are called "partner hotels."

Partner Hotels
Palm & Fountain Terrace Hotel
Hotel Emion Tokyo Bay
Oriental Hotel Tokyo Bay
Urayasu Brighton Hotel
Mitsui Garden Hotel Prana

There are no cost savings for staying at these hotels, which are slightly farther away and do not enjoy monorail access. Additionally, most of them pointedly advertise that only Japanese is spoken. While many workers at each hotel undoubtedly speak sufficient English for you to get by if necessary, these hotels should only be considered as a last resort. (Even then, a familiar hotel brand like Comfort Inn or Days Inn is not far away elsewhere in Tokyo. The English-speaking reception may be worth the extra commute.) Many business hotels may also be good choices. As a general rule, if the hotel has an online presence in English, the staff will be fluent in English.

Making Hotel Reservations

Often you can save money by booking your hotel room six months in advance, rather than waiting for the last minute. The first night of your stay can sometimes determine the room rate for the entire trip, and you might save money by making two separate reservations to get around this.

You can read about regular Disney hotels and official hotels on http://www.tokyodisneyresort.co.jp/en/index.html. There, you can also find price information and availability. Online room reservations can now be done online in English (or you can call long-distance to Japan). Some external websites like Orbitz may carry the official hotels or the partner hotels, as well.

Do not call the Disney hotels (Tokyo Disneyland Hotel, MiraCosta, Disney Ambassador) directly.

International visitors are required to book hotel rooms from the Reservation Center, a separate official agency. This is to your advantage, since employees speak perfect English at the Reservation Center. The same may not be true of the front desk at your hotel if you were to call directly.

The Tokyo Disney Resort Reservation Center is open from 9:00 a.m. to 9:00 p.m. Japan runs 14 hours ahead of Eastern Standard Time (13 hours during Daylight Savings Time) and 17 hours ahead of Pacific Standard Time (16 hours ahead during Daylight Savings Time). Here is the number to call, with the most common international codes already attached:

United States:	011-81-45-683-3333
United Kingdom:	00-81-45-683-3333
Australia:	0011-81-45-683-3333

To determine other international codes, visit:
http://www.timeanddate.com/worldclock/dialing.html

Your call will be answered by an automated phone tree that is, unfortunately, available only in Japanese. To navigate the phone tree quickly so that you can reach an English-speaking reservations agent, wait until the brief English recording comes on and press 9, then 1.

One way to avoid long-distance charges is to fax your reservation requests: (int'l code)-81-45-683-4049.

You will not be able to make reservations at the official hotels when speaking with the Tokyo Disney Resort Reservation Center, so plan instead to call them directly. Using the international codes noted above, call:

Tokyo Bay Maihama Hotel
(int'l code)-81-47-355-1222

Sunroute Plaza Hotel
    (int'l code)-81-47-355-1111
Tokyo Bay Hotel Tokyu
    (int'l code)-81-47-355-2411
Hilton Tokyo Bay
    (int'l code)-81-47-355-5000
Hotel Okura Tokyo Bay
    (int'l code)-81-47-355-3333
Sheraton Grande Tokyo Bay Hotel
    (int'l code)-81-47-355-5555

If your destination is the Hilton or the Sheraton, you'll be able to make reservations online by visiting the normal website for the corporate parent, or by calling their toll-free number for the United States.

If you are staying at one or more hotels off the Tokyo Disney Resort property entirely, make your reservations online at hotels.com or http://travel.rakuten.co.jp/en. Phone numbers for the partner hotels, if needed, can be located on the Resort's website at http://www.tokyodisneyresort.co.jp/en/index.html.

When making hotel reservations, remember to account for differences in time and be sure you understand the exact date on which you will arrive in Japan. For example, if you leave the East coast on a Thursday around noon, you will arrive in Tokyo on Friday at about three in the afternoon—the following day. All travelers from the United States will cross the international date line and lose a day going to Japan. You gain it back on the return trip, when you'll arrive in America at roughly the same hour (and on the same day) that you departed Japan.

Unlike most Western hotels, Japanese hotels often charge "per person" rather than "per room." This can add cost to the overall trip. Factor that into your budgeting from the beginning.

Large hotel chains may require a credit card number when making reservations. However, do not be surprised if the Disney and Japanese hotels create the reservation simply by trusting you, and without requiring a credit card to hold the room.

Room costs vary by season: top, peak, regular, and value. Top and peak seasons encompass much of the summer and the period around Christmas, as well as most weekends year-round. Regular season includes remaining weekends, plus most weekdays of May, September, October, November, and the first part of December. Value season is typically only on the weekends which fall during deep winter.

Also complicating matters is the fact that most hotel rooms in Japan are much smaller than comparable rooms in Western countries. Not every room can accommodate a family of four (in fact, some are optimized for just two people). Many rooms include pull-out beds or trundle beds to fit an extra person. Larger families may need to reserve two rooms. It is best to inquire about room sizes when you first phone the hotel or reservation center.

Making Airline Reservations

You should reserve and purchase your plane tickets only after you've determined your hotel bookings, though obviously you should research both before you commit to anything. One reason to book hotels first is that these reservations can be changed or cancelled later without a fee if it turns out that the airplane reservations don't match up. But making airplane reservations first and then changing them to fit hotel reservations will generally incur a fee, especially if you tried to save money by booking a non-refundable fare, as many people do.

Plan flights so that your arrival in Tokyo happens early enough that you can take the shuttle bus from the airport (more on this later), and so that you can avoid packed commuter trains.

If you're traveling from the United States, flight time is about 11 hours from the West coast or 14 hours from the East coast. Because you cross the International Date Line, this means you'll leave one morning and arrive the next morning, with an entire day vaporized. You'll recoup that day on your return trip, when you will quite literally "arrive even before you leave" according to your wristwatch.

Pay careful attention to that "lost day" as you plan your hotel stays in Japan. Make sure your arrival in Tokyo is set for the right day!

Check for flights on usual websites like Orbitz.com, but also on sites that specialize in international travel, such as I-ACE (http://www.iace-usa.com) and Lonely Planet (www.lonelyplanet.com).

Before You Leave

What to Pack

Naturally, you'll want to bring enough pants, shirts, underwear, and socks to last the duration of your trip. You may wish to plan on doing laundry while overseas, allowing you to only pack half the volume of clothes you'd otherwise need. This will enable you to leave larger luggage at home and bring only a midsize (or even small) suitcase—a definite advantage if you don't want to stick out like a sore thumb. Japanese travelers tend to have only small bags, and most trains and buses are not configured to handle large bags well. If you do bring a lot of clothes, you'll be better off with several small bags, particularly if you plan to move about the country apart from the Tokyo Disney Resort.

If you want to save space and bring fewer clothes, you might think you could wash your clothes right at the hotel. But at the Disney hotels, there are no coin-operated laundry machines. Dry cleaning is available at a high cost ($4 or so per item), so this may not be an option for visitors on a budget. The "official hotels," meanwhile, do offer Guest-operated laundry machines. Expect to pay the equivalent in yen of about $4 per load of laundry, which will include the powder and the drying cycle. You'll want to stockpile ¥100 coins before attempting this.

If you'll be traveling around the country and visiting temples (or private dwellings), be prepared to take off your shoes often. That will mean bringing a solid supply of good socks (without holes in them!) and you'll be glad if you have slip-off shoes without shoelaces. Also, be aware that shorts and revealing outfits (like low-cut blouses) are not appropriate for temples. Slip-off shoes will be unnecessary if the Tokyo Disney Resort is your only destination, since your shoes (and shirts) are required to stay on all of the time, except for certain high-end restaurants in Ikspiari.

Last, feel free to bring along your comfortable pajamas or the clothes you usually wear to bed. But for those moments after the shower, you can also use the fancy robe provided by the regular Disney hotels and the official hotels (just look in the closet).

Apart from clothing, here are some items you'll want to make sure you don't forget:

1. Valid passport. You should plan on 12-16 weeks of processing time to apply for a new passport. Start early!
2. Japan Railpass voucher (if you purchased one).
3. Jacket or sweatshirt, if traveling in any season other than summer. The early mornings and late evenings can get chilly, so some form of warm clothing is usually desirable. While day lockers are available, a small backpack offers greater convenience.
4. Umbrella, if traveling in summer or fall. It rains a lot in Japan! At the Tokyo Disney parks, good quality umbrellas are offered for sale at reasonable prices.
5. Map of the Tokyo train system (JR East) in English. These are readily available online. If you intend to use the subway instead (which system you'll be using should be decided before your trip), then also print that system.
6. Any needed chargers (for AA batteries, or cameras, or video cameras). Hint: If you're using American electronic devices, you may not need power adapters,

but you might need wall outlet adapters if your devices have the third plug (the ground plug) or have one (polarized) plug wider than the other. Japanese outlets have two identical slots. Electrical current varies a bit by region: in Tokyo and the east, expect 100 volts and 50 Hz; in the west (Kyoto, Hiroshima), expect 100 volts and 60 Hz. American devices likely will work, but they will charge more slowly.

7. Handkerchief or pocket Kleenex. Bathrooms outside the hotels and parks lack paper towels. You'll want something to dry your hands with.

8. Alcohol-based hand sanitizer. Public bathrooms often lack soap.

9. English-Japanese dictionary.

10. Any needed guidebooks, including this one.

11. Sunglasses. These can be surprisingly difficult to locate and purchase in Japan!

12. All the stuff you would normally bring on a vacation: airplane tickets, credit cards, camera, etc. Note that all hotels provide complimentary toiletries, including toothbrushes, toothpaste, comb, shampoo, and conditioner, since Japanese tourists tend not to bring their own along when they travel.

Parents traveling with children not yet potty-trained may wish to buy enough diapers for the vacation and pack them on the outbound trip. The extra space created by using up the diapers will come in handy later when souvenirs are purchased and must be carried back home. In the process you will spare yourself the need to buy more diapers, perhaps at inflated prices. For similar reasons, cans of infant formula can be packed in your bag before the trip over to Japan. Another useful item for parents to bring is a clear cover for their stroller in the event of rain. If you don't have room, though, you can purchase one at the Disney parks baby centers.

Money Matters

The value of the yen changes on a daily basis, but, in general, ¥100 is somewhat close to $1. If the dollar is "strong" in the year you visit, it could in fact be 1-to1, and you'd just need to move the decimal place to understand how much something costs (i.e., ¥2400 would cost $24).

If the dollar is "weaker" in the year when you visit, then ¥100 would be worth more like $1.20. Rather than do the math, you can just approximate. To estimate conservatively, especially considering there may be fees for conversion, you might want to figure on an extra dollar or two. Thus, when you see an item that costs ¥2400, you should ask yourself whether you would pay $28 for it.

If it helps, just ignore the last two zeros in the listed price, and you've got a very unspecific approximation of the cost in dollars.

As a good backup, plan to travel with three types of money available: cash, credit cards, and debit cards. You should always carry some yen with you; in some ways, Japan is still a cash-based country. The outdoor vending carts in the parks will not accept anything but cash, for instance. Many stores and smaller food stands off the beaten path will not accept credit cards, although those in and near the Tokyo Disney Resort usually do.

For credit cards, bring more than one with you—nothing would be worse than having your card declined in the middle of the trip, with no way to deal with the problem while overseas! If you booked a hotel outside of the Tokyo Disney Resort, remember that some online agencies (such as hotels.com) require that you bring and present the exact credit card used to secure the reservation.

Most vendors will accept Visa, MasterCard, and American Express, but not Diner's Club or Discover. If you should happen to have a JCB card, naturally that's accepted, since that bank calls Japan home.

An absolutely critical step before you travel is to phone your credit card companies and inform them of your travel plans, including the dates you will be in Japan. They will note this in their records, because once you start to make purchases in another country, the activity will raise automatic flags in card tracking systems. The credit card company often assumes your cards were stolen and freezes the accounts, leaving you high and dry. If they've been informed of your plans in advance, your accounts will remain unfrozen and will operate normally.

If a low credit card limit is an issue, or if you'll be traveling for an extended period of time, bring along or memorize your online payment log-in and password so that you can pay your monthly credit card bill from abroad (most hotels have a for-pay service to use the Internet for short periods of time). Note that you may have to visit your credit card company's website ahead of time to set up the ability to pay online directly from your bank. Do this before you leave on your trip!

Debit cards are useful as a way to obtain yen while overseas, since it's not always convenient to find a money conversion business (such as Thomas Cook). The conversion would have required cash in your normal currency, and these days debit cards have supplanted the need for traveler's checks. Debit cards are not commonly used at the Tokyo Disney Resort (unless the VISA logo is also present on the card), but they are becoming more common throughout the rest of Japan. You will find ATMs in the parks and at the hotels, and they host an extraordinarily wide variety of card systems, the most common American varieties being PLUS, Cirrus and Star. Be aware, though, that ATMs typically are only open certain times of the day, with the overnight hours certainly closed. Some only accept domestic cards (Bank of America cards, in particular, may not be accepted at Disney ATMs).

No matter how you slice it, converting money or using credit cards will result in a fee being charged to you. At currency conversion stands at the airport, the fee is built in to the conversion rate (if you were to buy $500 worth of yen and then sell it right back, you'd get less than $500 back, since they make money on both ends of the conversion). For debit cards and credit cards, it is possible that fees could be tacked on to every transaction, depending on your bank or credit card policies. VISA and MasterCard levy a 1% fee at a minimum, and some banks or credit card agencies add as much as an additional 2%. Some credit cards (most notably, the Capital One credit card) not only don't charge you 2% for foreign purchases, they even pay the 1% VISA charge for you, so the transaction is free of any fees.

Inside the Disney parks are counters where you can convert cash with no extra conversion fee, though you are limited in how much money you can convert to a few hundred.

Arrival and Transferring to Your Hotel

Arriving at Narita Airport

On the airplane trip over, you'll be handed a "landing" form and a customs declaration form. You'll only need one of each form for your entire family. Usually, announcements about how to fill these forms out are given over the loudspeaker in both English and Japanese, but the forms are pretty self-explanatory. If you're not carrying cargo or items to sell, you should have nothing to declare. The vast majority of tourists have nothing to declare. If you don't know the contact information for your hotel, simply provide as much information as possible (i.e., "MiraCosta Hotel, Tokyo Disney Resort" should be sufficient).

Keep these forms with you after you land. You'll be led from the arrival gate to an immigration zone, where an official will need to see your passport and your landing form. Because you are a visitor, expect to be fingerprinted and to have your photo taken. You may be asked to verify that you are visiting Japan for a vacation and/or the duration of your stay. A sticker and a stamp will be placed into your passport. Don't rip off the tear-away section of the sticker. This will be removed later by the customs officials.

In the next room, you'll find a luggage carousel. After you claim your bags, you pass through customs. Since most tourists have "nothing to declare," they simply hand over the customs form. Passengers are sometimes asked at random to open their luggage for a search to verify they do not have materials to declare. Assuming you bypass this search, you are likely to be free and in the main terminal a mere thirty minutes after your plane touches down. Never attempt to bring fake (knockoff) merchandise, such as licensed items or brand names, or pornographic material into the country (note: that means no photos or videos that show nudity). If found by a customs agent, you will be arrested on the spot!

Transferring to Your Hotel

Most flights from Western countries and Europe will deposit travelers in Terminal One. Northwest, Delta, and Continental (jointly known as Skyteam) land in the North Wing, while flights on the Star Alliance (United Airlines, US Airways and Air Canada) arrive in the South Wing. The One World Alliance (including American Airlines) lands at Terminal Two.

From the terminal, you'll arrange for transportation to the Tokyo Disney Resort. There is no official shuttle or transport offered by Disney itself, so you'll need to rely on alternatives. A common method at American airports is to rent a car, but, while this is theoretically possible, it's not advisable in Japan because of the high costs, difficult driving directions, and the fact that cars are driven on the left side of the street, rather than the right. Taxis exist, but they are prohibitively expensive. It would cost about two hundred dollars to take a cab from the airport to the Disney resort.

Perhaps the simplest method of all is Friendly Airport Limousine, which, despite its name, is a bus rather than a limousine. It offers a shuttle from the airport to both the regular Disney hotels and the official hotels. Simply approach the counter and let them know your hotel destination. The counter is located directly opposite your exit from customs.

Look for a sign labeled BUS TICKETS (sandwiched between "train tickets" and "hotel reservations"). They speak English well. Their website is www.limousinebus.co.jp/en.

You can expect a one-way journey to cost ¥2,400 (about $28/adult) and half that price for children 12 and under. You do not need to mention or purchase tickets for lap children; just for those who need their own seats. This shuttle is almost never full, and if there is room, you can spread out once you are on board. By default, children six and under are considered lap children, but if you want to be positive they can occupy their own seat, a ticket must be purchased. It's probably better to hope for open seats on the bus, which is likely to be the case most of the time, anyway. Important note: you'll only be able to buy tickets in cash, so convert some money to yen before you visit the counter.

One factor to consider with Friendly Airport Limousine is the schedule. A bus departs about once an hour, except for a few hours in the middle of the day when there are fewer.

However, there are no departures from the airport after 17:05. For those unfamiliar with 24-hour time, this is 5:05 p.m. I use 24-hour time in this book because it's visible universally in Japan, and you'll need to be familiar with it; just subtract 12 from any big number and you'll have the "normal" time. Because the last shuttle departs well before dark, you may need to consider other alternatives if you have a late-arriving flight. Or perhaps, knowing this, you may wish to book your flight so that you do arrive early enough for the shuttle. If you take the shuttle, budget around 60 minutes to arrive at the hotel, though traffic could make that estimate rise to 80 minutes or more. And don't be surprised if you stop at several partner and official hotels along the way.

In Terminal One, the bus stop for Disney hotels and official hotels is bus stop number seven, just outside the door. You will see lines painted on the cement at the bus stop; these are for placing your luggage so that attendants can place tags on your bags before the bus arrives. When they speak to you in Japanese, it's likely they are asking the name of your hotel so that this can be recorded. Note that this bus stop is used by other bus lines as well; the next bus to arrive is displayed on the digital read-out above the bus stop. Don't place your luggage or board a bus prematurely!

Play it safe by displaying your ticket to the attendant about five minutes before your bus is scheduled to arrive. Usually, hand gestures will suffice for communication about where to stand and what to do with your bags. Each bag will be tagged and you will be given a receipt. Keep the receipt safe because your bag will not be given to you at your destination without it.

The other major alternative to the shuttle is the train system. The subway doesn't reach Narita airport, but the trains do. Since the national railway system is called Japan Rail, the train stations are called JR stations. The JR station at Narita is downstairs. In Terminal One, descend two escalators to find yourself facing a Starbucks. To the left of the Starbucks is the entrance to the platforms. You'll need a ticket to go beyond these gates. A ticket can be purchased at nearby kiosks.

There are a few things to be aware of at these kiosks. First, there are competing systems next to each other. The Narita Express (NEX) train requires a special ticket, which is more expensive. It runs to Tokyo Station, the main train station for the city. From here, you'd have to take a different train down to the Disney area (specifically, the Keiyo line in the direction of Soga), and get off the train at Maihama. One neat trick: if you buy the Keiyo ticket at the same time as the NEX ticket, it's actually cheaper than a NEX ticket alone, since the fare is calculated as-the-crow-flies, and the final destination for the Disney parks is closer to the airport than Tokyo Station. But experienced travelers may not want to take the NEX train. It's not much faster than regular Japan Rail (JR) trains, and it costs much more.

Right next to the NEX kiosk is the kiosk for regular JR tickets. When you purchase tickets, you'll need to calculate the required fare, based on how far you're traveling. A large map overhead shows the network of JR trains and lines, but you'll notice that the stations are all denoted by Japanese characters, not English. One option is to purchase the least expensive fare and plan to pay extra (the difference up to the price you should have paid to begin with) when you arrive at your destination. This would be done by inserting your ticket into the "fare adjustment" machine located near the exit of every train station. But most first-time visitors are best served simply approaching the window and speaking to a person to buy the ticket to Maihama (pronounced "My-HA-muh")

Because the station map is in Japanese, it may be simpler to ask for help in English from the Information desk (halfway to the Starbucks from the escalator). Alternately, back upstairs next to the bus tickets is a place to purchase the same train tickets. But better yet, just use the shuttle bus described earlier.

If you plan to travel around the country beyond the Tokyo Disney Resort, it's possible you purchased a Japan Rail Pass (JR Pass) before you left for Japan. If so, this underground area is where you need to activate it. The JR Pass office is designated the "JR East Travel Service Center" by a bright green sign. From the escalator in Terminal One, turn right just before you get to Starbucks.

At this office, you can activate your JR Pass, but do this carefully if you plan to visit Disney first and travel later. It is possible to activate your pass for a date in the future, but be certain you specify you do not want the pass active until they day you need it. Otherwise, your JR Pass might be activated right away, and your seven (or 14) days of usage will begin immediately. If immediate activation is your goal, you can use this pass for the JR trains to get to Tokyo, and then to the Maihama station. Simply show the activated pass to the attendant at the JR gates, always located off to one side, and you'll be waved through. You do not need individual tickets to ride the "normal" JR trains; your pass is sufficient.

You need special reservations and tickets to ride the city-to-city bullet trains, known in Japanese as Shinkansen (note that your pass doesn't qualify for the very fastest bullet train, the Nozomi). To get those Shinkansen reservations, visit the JR East Travel Service Center. It's best to bring along a typed-up page with your desired itinerary, which helps with potential language issues since you can just hand them the paper. That will mean researching the trains, the network, and the departure times while still back at home; see http://www.jreast.co.jp/e/ for details. The official site has timetables at http://www.jreast.co.jp/e/timetables/index.html. However, an easier site to navigate and understand the train schedules is at http://www.hyperdia.com/. This is especially useful to see the name of the line you want, such as "Hikari" if you want to travel from Tokyo to Kyoto. Note that there are multiple Hikari trains throughout the day; for example, Hikari 401 only refers to a specific train that travels on that day. Other Hikari trains may travel the same route that day but at different times. It's advisable to make these reservations as soon as you arrive in Japan, even if they are for days in the future, and you might not use the JR pass until later. It's not possible to make reservations online, or before you arrive in the country. Also, your JR pass must be activated before you can make reservations (it suffices to have the pass "activated for future use").

If you activate a JR Pass right away, you can take the trains around the city, effective immediately, but it may not be clear (without speaking to someone) just which train to take. You can use the "Rapid Service" train if you don't have a JR Pass and need to buy a one-way ticket manually, but this kind of transaction is best accomplished with verbal help from the Information desk located nearby.

Don't pay any attention to a large billboard when you first descend the elevator, announcing an electric express to Tokyo separate from the train, bus, or subway lines. This refers to a private railroad system that is separate from the public transportation system. Just avoid it and deal only with the JR trains.

If you do take a JR train to Tokyo Station, you'll need to get off at the right station and change trains. If you're not paying attention, it may be possible to miss your station; it's always announced verbally, but you may not understand it. Watch for signs announcing which station you're arriving at, visible from inside the train as it pulls into the station and slows to a stop. Make this observation early. By the time the train stops completely, the signs on the platform might not be visible from where you're sitting on the train. You might find a schematic of the JR lines inside the train. Sometimes these have English station names in addition to the Japanese, and sometimes they do not. If you do see it in English (or have a map printed from home or a book which shows English) you can follow along as the train makes each stop. Note that some trains are "rapid" trains which don't stop at every station but save time by skipping some smaller stations. You might need to stay vigilant about which stations you've passed through, even if you didn't stop.

Once at Tokyo Station, exit the train and take the escalator to the main level (people with strollers will find elevators everywhere; there is no need to collapse the stroller). Once you're in the main concourse, revel in the chaos that is Tokyo Station for a few moments. People are going in every direction, many of them in a hurry, and it's a marvel there aren't collisions every few seconds. To find your next train, look to the signs in the ceiling. To get to the Tokyo Disney Resort, you want the Keiyo line, which has red signs. Follow those red signs to a completely different part of the train station. When you get close, follow the Keiyo sign that goes to either Soga or Fuchu-Hommachi Station. As this path ends at an elevator or escalator, look for Track Three or Four. Either one of those is the track you want to go to Tokyo Disney Resort (you can use either on this particular line because the Keiyo line STARTS here and either track will get you to Maihama).

On this train, stay put for five stations. The sixth stop should be Maihama, which is where you need to get off the train. Note: if the train you're on is a "rapid" train that makes fewer stops, Maihama will be the third stop, not the sixth. Of course, you could always just gaze out the windows to the right side of the train—when the Tokyo Disney Resort gets close, you'll have no trouble seeing it, and it will be obvious when to disembark.

Train announcements about which station is next come first in Japanese, then in English.

Note that on some trains, there are "green" cars, which are labeled that way so that people know this is a no-talking car.

If you're using a JR Pass, just show it manually to get out of the exit gates. If you purchased a one-way ticket, you'll need to insert the ticket stub again into the exit gate to get it to open for you. You've made it!

Taking the JR trains can be done by a non-speaker of Japanese, but it requires either experience with this kind of thing or a good deal of vigilance. Best of all, for simplicity, use the shuttle bus from the airport, rather than the trains. It costs more than the trains do, but it's much more direct, it's faster, and much less stressful.

Arriving at the Tokyo Disney Resort

At the Maihama JR station, you're within walking distance of several destinations. Tokyo Disneyland and the Tokyo

Disneyland Hotel lie in one direction, and the Disney Ambassador Hotel lies in the other direction. (The shopping zone Ikspiari lies between you and the Ambassador.) To go directly to Tokyo Disneyland or to the Tokyo Disneyland

Hotel, head off to your right as you exit the station into the fresh air. You'll use a bridge to pass over the street, and your destination will be clearly visible ahead.

The Disney hotels and the official hotels each have a shuttle bus (called a "Disneyland Resort Cruiser") at Maihama station that goes back and forth between here and that hotel. Going to your hotel could be as simple as finding the right one outside and climbing aboard.

But there's a better solution. There's a Welcome Center just outside the station to the left (the opposite direction of Tokyo Disneyland) for those staying at the Disney hotels. You can stop by here and learn all you need to know about park tickets and transportation to the hotel. The personnel speak great English. For the official hotels, the same location has a desk for each hotel downstairs. Just follow the winding staircase down for the same services.

You can not only learn about transportation, you also can buy park tickets here (see the section on buying tickets for more information). And you can check in here, so that you can skip lines at the main lobby. Best of all, these desks all offer free baggage delivery service: you leave your bags, and they'll be delivered to your room after you check in at the hotel. After dropping off your bags, taking the shuttle will be much easier. Just remember to bring the luggage receipt they will give you.

If you choose not to take the shuttle bus, you could walk to either Tokyo Disneyland Hotel or the Disney Ambassador Hotel, but the MiraCosta is too far away to walk, as are the official hotels. Your other option is to take the monorail, called the "Disneyland Resort Line." All Disney hotels are on the monorail loop except for the Ambassador, and all the official hotels are on the loop too. The monorail station is right next door to the Welcome Center on the second floor. You'll need to buy a one-way ticket: ¥260 for people 12 and older, and ¥130 for children six to eleven years old (under six is free). Insert the ticket into the subway turnstile to gain access to the station, and hold on to it when it comes back up to you, since you'll need it to leave the station at your destination. If you are staying at a Disney hotel (but not an Official hotel), you'll be given a pass to use the monorail for free after you check in. You'll need cash for this operation rather than a credit card.

The monorail travels in a giant loop around the TDR property. You start at Resort Gateway Station, and the next stop is Tokyo Disneyland and the Tokyo Disneyland Hotel. The stop after that is Bayside Station, which is the stop for all the official hotels. The next stop is Tokyo DisneySea and MiraCosta, and then the train returns to Resort Gateway Station. If you miss your stop, don't fret. The train makes an endless circuit, and you can simply disembark on the next pass. To leave the station of your choice, find the turnstiles, insert the same ticket used earlier, and the turnstile will open, although your ticket will not be returned.

Once you've found your hotel, follow the signs in English to the lobby or registration area. The staff who work the front desk at all these hotels speak excellent English. Some of them may well be the best English-speakers you'll find on your vacation! Early check in—where you can return later for your key—is allowed on every day except Sunday. Note that when you check in—either at the Welcome Center or at the hotel itself—you'll be required to submit your passport to be photocopied, in accordance with Japanese law. You'll also be asked to provide a credit card, which may be imprinted on an old-fashioned carbon imprint, and it's also likely you'll be asked to sign the imprint right away, even though it's still blank. This may be quite foreign to Western visitors, but it's perfectly safe.

If you still have your luggage with you, a bellhop may be called to take it to your room for you. In fact, you may be escorted to your room, even if you have no bags. The high level of service may tempt you into thinking you should hand out an especially nice tip when the bellhop leaves you at the room. But this is actually not acceptable, since tipping is not encouraged or even expected, and that's true of the whole country. Don't tip anyone, even at restaurants. The culture here revolves around the idea that good service is meant to bring its own rewards: if the customer goes away happy, he or she is all the more likely to return. Trying to tip a Japanese citizen is more likely to embarrass than to flatter or please.

When you get to your room, take the time to explore the bathroom. You'll likely find a high-tech toilet that warms up the seat as soon as it senses your weight and has buttons for "spray" and "bidet", both of which squirt a thin jet of warm water. You ought to give this a try—when in Rome, why not do as the Romans do? For some toilets, the stream of water will continue until you press the nearby STOP button. The "odor" button on the panel controls a small fan that draws air inward.

Pause also to check out the shower. The bathtub will seem familiar enough, if quite a bit deeper than you're used to (the Japanese love to soak in a tub of hot water). In many hotels, though, the shower zone occupies the rest of this room. Close the door, and you are already in the shower itself. There is no need for a curtain. The entire room is tiled and expected to get wet; in the shower area the water drains to one side under the tub (this is known as a "French drain"). Luxuriate in the fast, powerful spray from the showerhead, then use your soaps and shampoos before you climb in the tub for some simple soaking in plain hot water. The Japanese never bring soap into the bathtub, and they all share the same bathwater, not draining it until the last person has finished his/her soak.

Park Admission and Touring Plan

Buying Tickets

You can't purchase park tickets before your trip either at travel agencies or online. They are available at places like Disney stores, convenience stores around Japan, at the Main Entrance gates themselves, at the Welcome Center next to the Maihama JR station, and at your Disney hotel or official hotel. Of these options, the simplest and quickest is to buy your tickets at the hotel. That can be done on the day you enter the park or any date before then. Buying at the hotel means you'll have access to folks who speak English well. A second viable alternative is to buy tickets at the Welcome Center.

When you buy tickets, you'll be asked to specify the dates for which the tickets are good. If you are buying a multi-day pass, you will also be told to specify which park you want on which day, and this has to be decided in advance. The first two days must be for Tokyo Disneyland and Tokyo DisneySea (or the reverse), and then Day Three is a parkhopper day, when you can visit either park, or both parks on the same day. If you buy a four-day pass, the procedure is the same; only days 3 and 4 are parkhopper pass days. For those parkhopper days, there is no need to specify which park(s) you plan to attend. It's also important to note that your multi-day passes are for consecutive days only; you can't take any time off between days to do other things and then "restart" the multi-day ticket. You'll receive your actual tickets, not vouchers, right on the spot. Guard these well, and don't lose them! There are no passports for longer than four days, other than annual passes.

One great advantage to buying tickets when you first arrive is that you will be guaranteed admission to the park. During

peak seasons, the gates are often shut when the parks fill to capacity, particularly at Tokyo Disneyland. When that happens, visitors who bought tickets at travel agencies and convenience stores throughout Japan won't be allowed in, since their tickets are not date-specific. Your tickets purchased at the hotel, however, grant you priority admission to the parks.

Here are the ticket prices as of 2016:

	Ages 18+	Ages 12-17	Ages 4-11
1-day	¥7,400	¥6,400	¥4,800
2-day	¥13,200	¥11,600	¥8,600
3-day	¥17,800	¥15,500	¥11,500
4-day	¥22,400	¥19,400	¥14,400

There is a senior discount only for the one-day passport, for ¥6,700. All tickets are for single-park admission. However, on 3-day and 4-day passports, the third and fourth days are considered "parkhopper" days, as previously mentioned.

Note that your ticket options also include evening-only tickets you might consider for your first day at the resort, if jet lag isn't a major factor. On most weekdays, these are valid from 18:00 until closing. On weekends and holidays, they are valid from 15:00 until closing, which looks like a better deal until you remember that the parks are more crowded, and the lines are much longer, on the weekends. Expect to pay ¥4,900 for the weekend "Starlight" pass and ¥4,200 for the weekday "After Six" pass.

You can find current ticket price information on the official website: http://www.tokyodisneyresort.jp/en/ticket/

Transportation to the Park

Tokyo Disneyland is accessible by walking from the Tokyo Disneyland Hotel or from the Disney Ambassador Hotel (though the latter requires a much longer walk). Tokyo DisneySea is accessible by foot from the MiraCosta (and, with a longer walk, from the Disney Ambassador Hotel). Otherwise, you'll need transportation to the park.

The monorail costs money to use if you are not staying at a Disney hotel. The one-use ticket costs ¥250 for people 12 and older, and ¥130 for children six to eleven years old (under six is free). The one-day pass is ¥650, which costs considerably more than two of the one-way passes, so this only makes sense if you plan multiple trips. However, the multi-day passes make more financial sense. An adult will pay ¥1,400 for four days, an average of just ¥350 per day, with unlimited uses per day. The other advantage of passes is that you don't have to keep visiting the kiosks, which can sport long lines at many hours of the day.

If you have a daylong (or weekly, or monthly) transit pass to Tokyo that is good on subways and buses, this will also work for the monorail.

A free transportation solution is to take your hotel's shuttle to the park. One caution: these become crowded at certain times of the day, and strollers will have to be folded up. When it's very crowded, like at the closing of the park, expect standing-room-only crowds. At the official hotels, sometimes the shuttles only run to the monorail's Bayside station rather than all the way to the theme parks.

The Golden Rule: Start the Day Early

The title of this section says it all, but this really is the single most important factor in your enjoyment of the day, apart from the planning you did weeks and months ago. Tokyo DisneySea and Tokyo Disneyland become very crowded, very fast. That has particular implications for the rides perceived as especially desirable, where the lines spiral out of control almost right away. A delay of even five minutes at the start of the day will yield an additional wait in line of much more than five minutes; perhaps as many as twenty or forty. It is no exaggeration to say that people sprint to their favorite attraction when the gates first open, and although the bevy of smiling and waving Cast Members they pass by will occasionally rebuke them about running, it's done in a half-hearted fashion and has absolutely no effect on the sprinters. Amusingly, a small minority will rush inside the gates and forgo any attractions, preferring instead to accost the costumed characters in the entrance plaza. Lines for photographs form instantly.

It will do no good to sprint to dinner-show restaurants (Diamond Horseshoe, Tahitian Terrace) at the start of the morning; these no longer accept same-day reservations. Reservations must be made ahead of time. You could do it online only if you spoke Japanese; otherwise, visit a kiosk at a restaurant in-park once you arrive and arrange for a visit at a later day.

People line up before the gates open. If you arrive thirty minutes before park opening, you'll find about twenty or thirty people in each line ahead of you. By the fifteen minute mark, the lines will stretch back quite a distance, and there will be amazing crowds by the time the gates actually open. Plan on much longer lines during holidays and crowded periods; you should arrive a full hour before park opening on those days. Most Japanese visitors will wait out this line sitting patiently, but Disney handlers will occasionally urge those in line to edge ever closer to the people in front of them, in some cases violating what many Westerners see as personal space. Obviously, personal space issues are different in Japan (just ride the subway during rush hour to witness an extreme example of this). The Cast Members compact the line because they know it will stretch out too long as it is, and they want to leave room for everyone else yet to come.

In American Disney parks, there is sometimes a "rope drop" early in the morning, in which the turnstiles (and perhaps part of Main Street) open before the designated moment, but there is a rope to prevent anyone from going too far. There is no "rope drop" at Tokyo Disneyland and Tokyo DisneySea. At the Tokyo parks, the turnstiles simply don't open until the preordained time, though costumed characters may appear just inside the gates a few minutes early to build excitement.

The Golden Rule is simple. Start the day early, because everyone else is doing it. You might be tempted to sleep in, in order to attempt to reap some shorter lines at the end of the night, but with jet lag, it's unlikely you'll last that long. The probability of short lines is better in the morning than in the late evening, anyway. I found it profitable to wait in these pre-opening lines for 15-30 minutes before opening time. That didn't require waking up too early, but it still got us in position to hit some rides early and quickly, once the park opened.

The Disney Hotels and the Official Hotels allow patrons to participate in Extra Magic Hours (EMH). Use these! You can get a big jump on the day with early admission.

If you're looking for a park map in English, you won't find them at the turnstiles or at most stores in the parks, which is different from the American Disney theme parks. You'll need to visit Guest Relations to get one.

Options for Creating Your Touring Plan

A "touring plan" is simply the rough sketch of which attractions you'd like to see, and in what order. In general, this translates into simply ranking what's important to see, but there are exceptions to this rule, particularly regarding time savers like FASTPASS or the single-rider lines at Tokyo DisneySea (more on these ideas later). These complications mean you don't have to wait in the "normal" lines for those rides, so take that into account when you create your plan.

The first step is simply to have a plan. Many visitors don't, but this is a mistake. You lose valuable time, which is particularly crucial early in the morning, if you wait until you finish riding one attraction before deciding what to do next. Also, it's important to retain an overview of the day. You don't need to plan the day out to every last detail or down to the minute—that's probably overkill and will result in more stress, not less. But you will benefit from plotting a few moves ahead on a continuous basis, adjusting for crowd patterns as necessary. The FASTPASS tickets you obtain also may cause you to re-think priorities, especially if they have "return times" you hadn't counted on. In the era of FASTPASS, it's best not to move through the park in a simple clockwise (or counter-clockwise) fashion, hitting the rides as you come to them. Instead, craft a plan to zigzag across the park. It sounds counter-intuitive, because you lose time in the transit, but you'll more than make up that time by minimizing long waits. Here are some general rules to live by:

1. Hit the "biggest rides" early, usually defined as the newest or the most thrilling.

2. Use FASTPASS whenever possible on those biggest rides. If you grab a FASTPASS, don't wait in the Standby line to ride twice. You're losing valuable time. You might want to make an exception to that rule, however, for the most thrilling rides.

3. Remember, some of the "E-Ticket" rides can be visited later in the day, using FASTPASS (see the later section on FASTPASS for a discussion of which rides "run out" of tickets first, and which keep the tickets longer). A big caveat to this  rule: if the park is very crowded, FASTPASS everywhere will "run out" quickly, and you can't count on it for later in the day.

4. Zigzag through the park to hit your "E-Ticket" rides in your ranked order. Don't just move around the park methodically in a circle, stopping at each attraction, unless you're doing this in conjunction with a concerted FASTPASS plan.

5. Skip the smaller rides until later in the day, especially those that will not have tremendously long lines even in the crowded middle part of the day. The Jungle Cruise and Western River Railroad have shorter lines after dark and are more exciting then in any event.

6. As a counter-argument to the previous item, you may walk past a completely empty attraction in the early part of the day. If there is literally no line and the ride won't take long, you are losing only a few minutes by riding it immediately, so it may make sense to stop after all. Plan to be flexible, based on the conditions you encounter.

7. If you're familiar with the rides in other Disney parks, skip those which are identical (or nearly so), such as Dumbo or the Fantasyland dark rides. This gives you more time for rides which are radically different, like Pooh's Hunny Hunt or Monsters Inc. Hide and Go Seek.

8. Speaking of the Fantasyland dark rides, many have surprisingly long lines, which should either encourage you to prioritize those attractions, or allow them to fall from your list, depending on your preferences (and whether you have kids). Many rides may be fundamentally the same, but have scenes presented in a different order and with unique details. Such minor enhancements are true also of Splash Mountain, where low-hanging vines create a more intimate atmosphere, and the Haunted Mansion, where one book in the library turns its own pages and another book walks along the floor.

Here's one sample touring plan:
   a. Monsters Inc. Hide and Go Seek (standby)
   b. Monsters Inc. Hide and Go Seek (obtain FASTPASS)
   c. Splash Mountain (standby)

d. Big Thunder Mountain Railroad (standby)
e. Pooh's Hunny Hunt (obtain FASTPASS)
f. Space Mountain (standby, with a wait)
g. Pooh's Hunny Hunt (use FASTPASS)
h. Turn to smaller attractions for the middle and latter part of the day

A final variable to consider is staying late, perhaps until park closing. Crowds die down somewhat after darkness sets in, and especially after nighttime parades and fireworks. This is particularly true in the extreme corners of the parks (farthest from the main entrance). Though the premium rides will still sport a line, the wait will be measurably shorter. And a few rides may have no line at all, such as Jungle Cruise or Pirates of the Caribbean. You may even find that the "late night advantage" is even better than the "early morning advantage" for a majority of rides. The big exceptions are Toy Story Mania and Monsters Inc—you'll want to be in the park early for those.

For visitors with mobility issues, you should know the parks are crowded, and visitors in wheelchairs are not nearly as common as the American parks. The little scooters called Electronic Convenience Vehicles (ECVs) are very common in American parks, but much less commonly seen here. The vast majority of visitors are able-bodied and may find an ECV a strange sight to behold. Visitors who do use a wheelchair will find the parks to be handicapped-accessible, and the visitor centers stock helpful booklets in English about accessibility.

Attraction Descriptions

Tokyo Disneyland Overview

Laid out like the familiar Disneyland and Magic Kingdom in the United States, Tokyo Disneyland features themed lands organized around epochs in history or geographic areas. Some visitors have likened it to a perfected Magic Kingdom concept, and indeed, one can see Orlando's Magic Kingdom as the immediate creative ancestor of this park.

World Bazaar

Rather than Main Street, Tokyo Disneyland features World Bazaar, partly because the notion of an American town at the turn of the 20th century wouldn't play as well in Japan. Though the theme is different, the result is similar: a collection of shops and restaurants heralds the land everyone is funneled through for both entering and leaving the park. One major difference is that the entire area is covered, since it rains so much in Japan, and this provides a much more convenient shopping experience. You can also dart directly into Tomorrowland or Adventureland via a side street not far from the main entrance.

You may think there are no attractions per se in World Bazaar, except perhaps the Omnibus, which moves up and down the street, but the Disney Gallery and the Penny Arcade are worth a quick peek.

Tomorrowland

Tomorrowland is meant to celebrate the future, as well as visions of the future that never came to be. The land, as a whole, mixes science fantasy and science fact, with attractions reflecting both kinds of futurism.

Monsters Inc Hide and Go Seek: A 2009 addition to Tokyo Disneyland, this dark ride has amazing animatronics and always sports a long line. FASTPASS will run out here very quickly.

Space Mountain: A roller coaster in the dark, this Space Mountain is a duplicate of the ride in Anaheim's Disneyland, though the show elements and theming are different following an extensive refurbishment in 2007, and there is no onboard audio. No inversions. Riders must be 102 cm (40 inches).

Buzz Lightyear's Astro Blasters: Resembling the rides in Anaheim and Orlando, Astro Blasters is a slow-moving dark ride with numerous show elements from the *Toy Story* movies. Ride vehicles are equipped with laser blasters, and patrons shoot at targets throughout the attraction, even moving their vehicles to adjust the aim. Like the Anaheim variant, this one features blasters that can be held in your hand, rather than being anchored to the ride vehicle.

Star Tours: The Adventures Continue: A flight simulator for an entire cabin of people, Star Tours mixes realistic motion and a viewscreen full of action from the *Star Wars* universe to provide thrills for all ages, with different episodes each time you ride. Similar to American versions.

StarJets: A futuristic twist on the carnival "spinner" type of attraction, this ride takes place high in the sky.

Captain EO: This 3D sci-fi movie follows Michael Jackson as he brings music and dance to a distant world and transforms it into a paradise. Identical to U.S. versions.

Grand Circuit Raceway: Children can drive their own race cars through a twisting course in this miniature automobile attraction.

Tomorrowland Hall: This facility next to Space Mountain is where you go (early in the day) to enter the lottery for a ticket to the castle stage shows. We found that our type of ticket seemed to "win" all the time.

Toontown

Posited as a city populated by cartoon characters, Toontown is based on the fictional world of *Who Framed Roger Rabbit*, and features three districts: downtown, the civic center, and residential. Little visitors who push and prod all sorts of interactive buttons and levers throughout the land often are rewarded with sound effects and other zany reactions.

Roger Rabbit's Car Toon Spin: A dark ride with a (literal) twist, this ride affords patrons the opportunity to not just witness the events of *Who Framed Roger Rabbit*, but to play along by spinning their own ride vehicles. Completely identical to the version in Disneyland's Anaheim.

Gadget's Go Coaster: Cobbled together from bits of discarded tools and trash, this coaster is themed to the inventor Gadget from the 1990s Disney Afternoon cartoon, *Chip 'n Dale Rescue Rangers*.

Mickey's House and Meet Mickey: Walk through Mickey's house, watching for jokes in the props all around you, and finally take a photo with a costumed Mickey afterward. Expect very long lines—up to two hours.

Goofy's Paint 'n Play: The former Goofy's Bounce House is now a chance to use Toy Story-style cannons to launch virtual paint at the walls.

Minnie's House: You can't meet Minnie and take a photo with her, but you can walk through her house and play with many interactive props.

Chip 'n Dale's Treehouse: Children can pretend to be the famous chipmunks here, playing on a slide or in a pit full of balls.

Donald's Boat: All the props on this play boat are interactive, and children can explore all over the place.

Fantasyland

Home to attractions and shows that honor Disney's animated characters, Fantasyland offers everyone the chance to see their favorite characters in their own settings.

Pooh's Hunny Hunt: Explore the Hundred Acre Wood in a rolling honey pot. This unique ride is not like its United States counterparts; it is a technological masterpiece. Your honey pot ride vehicles, controlled by a GPS system, glide across the floor with no tracks, and on many occasions it looks like you'll hit other ride vehicles. The staging, the animatronic performers, the music, and the ride system leave visitors shaking their heads in wonderment.

Haunted Mansion: A slow-moving dark ride through an eerie house, the Haunted Mansion is populated by numerous ghostly special effects. Not much different in execution than the Orlando version of the same attraction, apart from a few bonus effects.

It's a Small World: Travel on slow-moving boats past animatronic dolls meant to represent the children of the world, singing a common anthem.

Cinderella's Fairy Tale Hall: A walk-through exhibit in the castle, using artwork and mini-dioramas to tell the Cinderella story.

Mickey's Philharmagic: A 3D movie that shows Donald Duck racing through several Disney animated films. Identical to Orlando's version.

Peter Pan's Flight: This is a dark ride with a twist; the ride vehicles are suspended from the ceiling, and you fly over models of London and then Neverland. Slightly different scenes from the American versions.

Dumbo the Flying Elephant: An outdoor spinning ride that has the added fun of letting patrons control how high they want their elephant vehicles to fly.

Snow White's Adventures: This dark ride takes visitors through scenes from the Disney movie. Similar to versions in the United States.

Pinocchio's Daring Journey: Another dark ride based on a movie, and identical to the version in Anaheim's Disneyland.

Alice's Tea Party: Spin your own tea cup as fast or slow as you'd like.

Castle Carrousel: This outdoor carousel has plenty of horses for all riders.

Critter Country

The mystique of the American South and part of its heritage of exploration are highlighted in this land.

Splash Mountain: A log ride through the American South, Splash Mountain tells the stories of Br'er Rabbit taken from *Song of the South*. The final drop is quite long and steep. Both the queue and ride differ from American versions, and are more lavishly produced, with low-hanging vegetation providing a cozier feel. Riders must be 90 cm (35 inches) tall.

Beaver Brother's Explorer Canoes: Another way to navigate around the Western River, the canoes offer visitors a chance to provide forward motion the old-fashioned way.

Westernland

Celebrating the Wild West and all things American, especially from the 1800s, Westernland captures the look and feel of a country pushing out onto its frontiers, highlighting a spirit of exploration and pioneering.

Big Thunder Mountain Railroad: Themed like a runaway mine train, this roller coaster barrels through canyons and tunnels, and past animals. The track layout is entirely different from the versions of this ride in Anaheim and Orlando. Look for surprises especially toward the end. No inversions. Riders must be 102 cm (40 inches) tall.

Country Bear Theater: This musical revue by animatronic bears celebrates the backwoods South. Songs are in Japanese. For some shows, the songs are original to this attraction, rather than duplicated from shows in the United States.

Mark Twain Riverboat: Ply the Western River in this paddlewheel boat as it slowly makes its way past Indians and mining settlements.

Westernland Shootin' Gallery: This shooting gallery not only offers the chance to test your aim, you will also win a collectible prize with a perfect score. Targets are easier to hit than you might anticipate, reflecting the Japanese desire not to disappoint.

Adventureland

From steamy jungles to scurrilous pirates, Adventureland explores the tropical climates of the world and highlights the exotic.

Pirates of the Caribbean: A slow boat ride with a significant drop down a waterfall, Pirates of the Caribbean adheres to a storyline and layout similar to Anaheim's version (minus the Captain's Quarters), with Captain Jack Sparrow and his comrades running amok amid caves, a fort, and a city.

Western River Railroad: Three cheerfully-colored locomotives, powered by live steam, chug around the woods and rivers in Westernland. One dramatic show scene is not visible from the outside, but surprises visitors near the end of the ride. Note that the Tokyo version is not transportation around the park; you exit from the same station where you boarded.

Jungle Cruise: This slow boat ride down exotic rivers of the world passes by animatronic critters and ruined temples. The spiel is delivered in Japanese by a live skipper.

Enchanted Tiki Room: The Tiki Room features animatronic birds, flowers, and wooden tiki gods in a musical show. This version has all-new songs that are different from both Anaheim and Orlando, and it features Stitch, a popular character in Japan.

Swiss Family Robinson Treehouse: The Treehouse is a walk-through attraction where patrons can visit the adopted home of a family as seen in the movie *The Swiss Family Robinson*.

Tokyo DisneySea Overview

Built as a counterpoint to Tokyo Disneyland, Tokyo DisneySea (witness the contrast even in the names) celebrates the oceans of the world and the waterways which have helped to shape the evolution of culture over time. Water is part of the theme for every "land" here (in truth, they are called ports, not lands, at this park).

Mediterranean Harbor

From the port cities of Italy to the galleons that explored the Mediterranean, this area commemorates the European heritage of life on the sea. The central lagoon for the park can be found here, and it forms the venue for the major shows.

Fortress Explorations: Don't skimp on time dedicated to wandering around this stronghold and its associated rooms. Thematic elements await you in almost every chamber. Four different maps, available also in English, explain the rooms of the attraction and will greatly enhance your experience here. Look for the maps at the attraction or at Guest Services.

There's a Leonardo DaVinci game in this area similar to Sorcerers of the Magic Kingdom (Guests tap items to certain spots to trigger a real-world physical effect), but it's in Japanese only.

Venetian Gondolas: Your Japanese skipper will pole you around the lagoon and even sing Italian opera! Often features very long lines.

American Waterfront

Modeled after the 1920s in the United States, the American Waterfront combines luxury, mystique, and greed into a conglomerate vision of a complex society functioning on multiple levels.

Tower of Terror: Adventurer Lord Hightower has made his way around the exotic corners of the world, and your visit to his hotel can yield significant shrieking, as visitors are dropped in a free-fall down the elevator shaft. Lavish in details, this version has a totally different storyline and theming than American versions. Don't take your eye of the statue of Shiriki Utundu in the preshow, where you will witness an amazing illusion. Riders must be 102 cm (40 inches) tall.

Toy Story Mania: Shoot at onscreen targets and compete with your fellow riders in this digital traveling carnival game. This ride gathers an early morning crowd.

S.S. Columbia: Explore the full-sized transatlantic steamer on your own terms, pausing at the lounges and restaurants when appropriate, and visiting the bow section for a vista of the park and Tokyo Bay.

Turtle Talk With Crush: Kids will enjoy the cartoon Crush on the viewscreen, who interacts with us as though the screen was a window to the open water beyond. Note that the action occurs in Japanese, not English, and since it is live, there is no automated translation available. Located inside the S.S. Columbia, and similar to American versions of the show.

Big City Vehicles: Travel to Cape Cod in style, either as a passenger in an open-air vehicle, or as an obvious prisoner on the paddy wagon. The vehicles travel very slowly. If you're in a hurry, walking would be faster.

DisneySea Electric Railway: A railroad to Port Discovery, this attraction recalls elevated rail systems that were famous in Chicago and New York City. Listen for the artificially created screech of rail wheels on the metal track.

DisneySea Transit Steamer Line: Travel around the areas of Tokyo DisneySea by stopping at every boarding zone. (A note about the Transit Steamer Lines: there are three boarding stations, but only the station in the American Waterfront makes a complete circuit without stopping. Also, all the steamers shut down during the lagoon shows.)

Cape Cod

Harkening back to a simpler time in America, Cape Cod recalls the reliance upon the sea for sustenance and commerce, with a correspondingly slower pace of everyday life. The only attraction here is the show Donald's Boat in the Cape Cod Cook-Off Restaurant.

DisneySea Transit Steamer Line: Travel around the areas of Tokyo DisneySea by stopping at every boarding zone. (A note about the Transit Steamer Lines: there are three boarding stations, but only the station in the American Waterfront makes a complete circuit. Also, all the steamers shut down during the lagoon shows.)

Big City Vehicles: Travel to the American Waterfront in style, either as a passenger in an open-air vehicle, or as an obvious prisoner on the paddy wagon. The vehicles move very slowly.

Mysterious Island

Jules Verne's novels provide the inspiration for Mysterious Island, the volcanic home base for the sub Nautilus, and the entire area adheres to the theme of mankind imprinting its metallic wonders on the harsh landscape of nature.

Journey to the Center of the Earth: One of the premier attractions in Tokyo DisneySea, Journey to the Center of the Earth takes visitors into the heart of a volcano, through the mineral deposits of a mine, and down into the realm of a monster. The ride sometimes zooms through fast portions, loud effects, and a brief drop. Similar in ride style to Orlando's Test Track. Riders must be 117 cm (46 inches) tall.

20,000 Leagues Under the Sea: An exploration of the bottom of the ocean and eventual discovery of an undersea kingdom, this attraction magically makes dry sets look like the sodden bottom of the ocean. Narration is in Japanese but, oddly enough, even by English-speaking patrons may find they get the gist of the story. There is one element of the story which may not make sense to English-speakers. After a power loss, it's deep sea creatures which are pushing us back to the surface.

Mount Prometheus: You may not consider the volcano an attraction unto itself, but when it erupts (every thirty minutes), you'll certain pay attention!

Port Discovery

"Future Fantasy" might be a good way to describe the optimistic streak on display at Port Discovery, an area consumed by visions of both harnessing and respecting the natural forces around us. In this area, science leads the way toward understanding the world we see.

Aquatopia: A gentle ride that moves throughout an inch-deep lagoon, zooming toward whirlpools and waterfalls, Aquatopia has the cachet of technology without a deep storyline. It offers little suspense, however, so it often has small lines. During the summer, a variation called the "wet course" will cause your vehicle to hit every water trap head-on.

DisneySea Electric Railway: A railroad to the American Waterfront, this attraction eschews deep thematic elements for its transportation benefits.

Lost River Delta

Water and rivers can lead us into uncharted territory, and the Lost River Delta delights in exposing ancient cultures and temples uncovered as a result.

Indiana Jones Adventure and the Crystal Skull: Explore a South American ruined temple in a jeep that bounces realistically. Identical to Anaheim's version except for a few thematic elements. However, unlike Anaheim's version, there are no alternate ride experiences. Riders must be 117 cm (46 inches) tall.

Raging Spirits: This roller-coaster has minimal theming and only a couple of interesting atmospheric effects. Riders must be 117 cm (46 inches) tall. There is also a maximum height limit of 195 cm (6 feet, 4 inches). This is the only roller-coaster at Tokyo Disney Resort to have a loop.

DisneySea Transit Steamer Line: Travel around the areas of Tokyo DisneySea by stopping at every boarding zone. (A note about the Transit Steamer Lines: there are three boarding stations, but only the station in the American Waterfront makes a complete circuit. Also, all the steamers shut down during the lagoon shows.)

Mickey Meeting Trail: A place to meet characters near the bridge to Port Discovery.

Arabian Coast

The Middle Eastern variety of life can be found in this area, from the literary traditions of Sindbad to the Disney versions of Aladdin and the Genie.

Sindbad's Storybook Voyage: Changed in 2007 to a musical adventure with a catchy theme song, this slow-moving boat attraction recalls the minimalist animatronics of It's a Small World while exploring the stories of Sindbad. However, the animatronics are far more advanced than those in It's a Small World.

Magic Lamp Theater: The story of Aladdin and the Genie is explored here in this combo live-action, 3-D movie that tells the familiar narrative, but also manages to probe new ground. English-speakers can request hand-held translation devices at the front of the attraction. Be sure you pay attention to the preshow, when a verbose robotic cobra will dazzle you while setting the scene.

Caravan Carousel: This unique two-story indoor carousel offers visitors the chance to ride exotic animals and perhaps even the Genie himself.

Jasmine's Flying Carpets: A Dumbo-style spinner near Sindbad's Storybook Voyage.

Mermaid Lagoon

Most of the land is dominated by Trident's Kingdom, an "undersea" zone with rides for children and rich theming with aesthetics that will leave even skeptics weak-kneed with awe.

Mermaid Lagoon Theater: Professional-level stunts and effects characterize this show deep in Trident's Kingdom. Not to be missed.

Scuttle's Scooters: A ground-level spinner that will leave children screaming for more, Scuttle's Scooters sits outside Trident's Kingdom and often sports less of a line than you'd expect.

Flounder's Flying Fish Coaster: An outdoor coaster with minimalist theming, this attraction will satisfy little tots, while leaving teenagers hungry for more.

Ariel's Playground: Not to be missed is this playground, which combines multiple sets and themed areas into an interactive, "run-anywhere" space. A free map will help you navigate.

Blowfish Balloon Race: An indoor spinner ride, this attraction is notable for the high level of theming in its queue.

The Whirlpool: This ride takes two vehicles and moves them in a quick figure-8 motion to create the illusion of a whirlpool.

Jumpin' Jellyfish: The drop-tower concept for kids, Jumpin' Jellyfish doesn't overdo it on thrills and opts instead for a gentle experience. No height restriction.

Ariel's Greeting Grotto: Located outside Trident's Kingdom (and almost in the Arabian Coast), this zone provides a simple way to meet Ariel and take a picture with her. Sometimes sports long lines.

Ride and Show Recommendations

This section was written while keeping in mind that some readers may want to be surprised and not know exactly what to expect in each ride. These rankings tell you what the author considers worthwhile without saying why. The rankings presume that readers are already familiar with the American versions of these rides, if any exist.

One important observation: unlike the American parks, Tokyo Disney parks utilize the summer months to refurbish attractions, so practically every year one of the "big" rides is offline for the summer.

Tokyo Disneyland Attractions

Here are the don't-miss attractions, listed in order (obviously, this is a subjective ranking):

1. Pooh's Hunny Hunt
2. Monsters Inc. Hide and Go Seek
3. Big Thunder Mountain
4. Space Mountain
5. Splash Mountain
6. Haunted Mansion (Holiday version)
7. Pirates of the Caribbean
8. Haunted Mansion (regular version)
9. Buzz Lightyear's Astro Blasters
10. Star Tours: the Adventures Continue
11. The Enchanted Tiki Room (contains Stitch)
12. It's a Small World (Holiday version)

Here is a list of second-tier rides, many of which are essentially the same as the U.S. versions, or which perhaps exhibit only small differences. These are also provided in ranked order:

13. It's a Small World (regular version)
14. Western River Railroad
15. Jungle Cruise
16. Cinderella's Fairy Tale Hall
17. Country Bear Theater
18. Mark Twain Riverboat
19. Peter Pan's Flight

20. Snow White's Adventures
21. Pinocchio's Daring Journey
22. Roger Rabbit's Car Toon Spin
23. Tom Sawyer Island
24. Swiss Family Treehouse
25. Beaver Brothers Explorer Canoes

Finally, rides you can skip if you need to maximize your time, because they are either wholly unremarkable, or entirely the same as the U.S. versions:

26. Mickey's Philharmagic
27. Grand Circuit Raceway
28. Dumbo the Flying Elephant
29. Alice's Tea Party
30. Castle Carrousel
31. Captain EO
32. StarJets
33. Gadget's Go Coaster
34. Mickey's House and Meet Mickey
35. Goofy's Bounce House
36. Minnie's House
37. Westernland Shootin' Gallery
38. Chip 'n Dale's Treehouse
39. Donald's Boat

Tokyo DisneySea Attractions

Here are the don't-miss attractions, listed in (subjective) ranked order:

1. Tower of Terror
2. Journey to the Center of the Earth
3. Indiana Jones Adventure: Temple of the Crystal Skull
4. Sindbad's Storybook Voyage
5. 20,000 Leagues Under the Sea
6. Toy Story Mania

7. Mermaid Lagoon Theater
8. Aquatopia
9. Magic Lamp Theater

Here is a list of second-tier rides:

10. DisneySea Transit Steamer Line
11. DisneySea Electric Railway
12. Fortress Explorations
13. Big City Vehicles
14. Scuttle's Scooters
15. Flounder's Flying Fish Coaster
16. Caravan Carousel

Finally, rides you can skip if you need to:

17. Raging Spirits
18. Venetian Gondolas
19. Ariel's Playground
20. Blowfish Balloon Race
21. The Whirlpool
22. Jumpin' Jellyfish
23. Ariel's Greeting Grotto

Shows and Parades

There are smaller shows in more intimate venues that you may decide to skip—I didn't see many of them myself until my fourth or fifth day in their respective parks—such as the shows in the castle forecourt, at the Mediterranean harbor, or at the Columbia dock. Likewise, you shouldn't feel compelled to seek out the street-level interaction, such as the roaming magician, or the band of apparent custodial workers who will break out instruments and start dance routines. Just enjoy these when you stumble across them.

But you should make a special effort to see the marquee shows and parades. Chief among them is Tokyo Disneyland's nighttime parade, the Tokyo Disneyland Electrical Parade: Dreamlights. This is an updated version of the American classic, with the familiar musical score accompanying many all-new floats. It features modern technology and some startlingly good special effects.

For a front-row view of the eye-popping nighttime floats, spend a full hour holding down a spot. An announcement makes public the policy that visitors are welcome to spread  out plastic sheets, almost like picnic blankets, starting one hour before showtime. Many Japanese families have these on hand, and they use them at other events besides the theme park. They remove shoes when they step on the sheets. Wonderfully, there is little "encroachment" by latecomers trying to get a good view of the show, and people don't inch closer as showtime draws near, as is the case at other Disney parks. They simply keep their distance as dictated by the plastic blankets.

Areas that fill up quite fast for Dreamlights include the central plaza and the parade's starting point near It's a Small World. However, the parade is so popular, the remaining areas on the route fill up not long afterward. If you arrive with fifteen minutes or less to go until showtime, expect to be standing far in the back, several rows away from the front. If your timing is right, you may be the first row of people standing, with everyone in front of you sitting down, so your view could still be excellent.

Other parades at Tokyo Disneyland are worth watching. During your visit there may be a daytime parade and perhaps a few "cavalcades," or mini-parades, that might seem, in theory, to be unremarkable. But Tokyo Disneyland parade floats are large, intricate, and fresh (seldom re-used), and the high energy is always accompanied by first-rate music. As a result, even the shorter cavalcades are well worth watching. But don't waste time holding a spot for these. Just line up a few minutes before they come rolling along.

There are special parades for summer (when floats liberally spray the audience with water), Halloween, and the Christmas season. During these times, the normal daytime parade may not run, though the nighttime Dreamlights will always run.

There are two prominent stage show venues: the castle forecourt and the Showbase amphitheater in Tomorrowland. Both are surprisingly crowded, but the shows are worthwhile, particularly if you have multiple days to explore the parks. The shows fill up very quickly. The seats for these shows (plus Big Band Beat in TDS) are awarded by lottery. Inquire at the show location about obtaining a ticket for the lottery.

The fireworks are good, but very brief and not as spectacular as their sister shows in California and Florida. You won't need a prime viewing location for the fireworks, and you won't need to reserve a spot at all. Just look up at the right moment, making sure there aren't tall obstructions. Fireworks are visible above both parks, but you may want to choose a spot that is not right next to buildings or trees. To do that effectively, you have to know where the fireworks are launched. They explode behind Splash Mountain, so, inside Tokyo Disneyland, be sure to keep that part of the sky in clear view. The actual launch zone is between the parks, and since Tokyo DisneySea was built later and oriented differently, there is no attraction at the spot you need to look toward. In the front half of the park, look above the aqueduct ruins, while at the Mermaid Lagoon entrance, look above Ariel's meet-and-greet spot.

Those who are not impressed by fireworks may find this to be an excellent opportunity to visit attractions, because the lines shorten perceptibly during the nighttime entertainment.

Tokyo DisneySea's main nighttime show is Fantasmic!, an adaptation of the show by the same name seen in the United States. It can be seen relatively well from all sides. A water-side location requires at least a 45-minute wait. Keep wind direction and ash fallout in mind when choosing a spot. Some visitors line up an hour before the show, and many stay seated the entire performance, so you might be expected to do the same. If arriving only 15 minutes before showtime, try the bridges near the volcano for second-row viewing.

One crowd-pleasing show at Tokyo DisneySea, named Big Band Beat, is not centrally located, and thus may escape the attention of some visitors. That's a shame, since the Big Band Beat is top-quality entertainment for thirty minutes, done old-style with show-stopping musical numbers, large casts, and synchronized dancing. Many repeat visitors consider it a

"don't-miss" attraction. It's located opposite the Electric
Railway in the vicinity of the Tower of Terror, in the
Broadway Music Theatre. You need tickets for this attraction;
there is no "standby" option for each performance.

There's also Mystic Rhythms, a great show in the Hangar
Theater in Lost River Delta, if you have the time. Back at
Tokyo Disneyland, Slue Foot Sue's Diamond Horseshoe has
two different shows, as does the Tahitian Terrace. A visitor
with a tight schedule might reasonably skip these smaller
shows, but if your schedule allows for it, they will be well
worth your time.

Maximizing FASTPASS

FASTPASS Definition

FASTPASS is a free ride-reservation system only found at high-demand rides. You insert your park admission ticket into a kiosk at the entrance to an attraction, and you receive a ticket in return, on which is printed a Return Time some point in the future. You are free to wander away and ride other attractions in the meantime. When the Return Time arrives (or at any time thereafter), you come back to the attraction and join the FASTPASS line, which is very short and served first, so if there is a line at all, it will move rapidly. Within a few minutes, you'll be on the

ride. By the way, each person has to hold their own FASTPASS ticket (not really enforced in the United States, but it is here).

No one is forced to use FASTPASS; you can always ride the attraction the usual way by waiting in line. At these attractions, the "normal" line has been renamed the Standby line. But consider: because there are other people returning to the ride in the FASTPASS line, they get served first, meaning that the Standby line is often stagnant for extended periods of time, and even a short line may take a long time.

If you aren't using FASTPASS, you are placing yourself at a distinct disadvantage, because every single person around you is doing it, and your Standby wait times on the big rides are longer as a result. At the parks in the United States, this is less true, where FASTPASS realistically might be considered only one option among many, but at Tokyo Disney Resort, the FASTPASS tickets will "run out" for every attraction on busy days, usually by mid-afternoon. For the really desirable attractions, they "run out" by noon, or even earlier.

Where to Use FASTPASS

By word of mouth and previous experience, Japanese patrons know which of the rides to visit first, and which of the rides never gain much of a line. This section was designed to level that playing field somewhat, so you, too, will know how to maximize your use of FASTPASS.

At Tokyo Disneyland, Monsters Inc. Hide and Go Seek is the big draw. Within minutes of opening, the Return Time jumps

forward an hour, and there is a big line just to get a FASTPASS. Often, by noon the last FASTPASS has been issued for the day. Every second counts! Get to Monsters Inc. as fast as you possibly can when the park first opens.

After Monsters Inc, Pooh's Hunny Hunt is the most popular FASTPASS attraction. Do not miss that attraction, for its innovative use of ride vehicles. After Pooh, it's Buzz that attracts the most FASTPASS interest. Visitors familiar with the American version of Buzz may benefit from using the FASTPASS for the thrill rides instead, since Splash Mountain, Big Thunder, and Space Mountain all run out of tickets by mid-afternoon. An experienced FASTPASS user may wish to obtain a Pooh FASTPASS and then ride one of the big thrill rides using its Standby line right away, while morning crowds are still extremely light, eliminating a need to get a FASTPASS for that ride later on.

If you've never been to a Disney park before, you may wish to use FASTPASS on the Haunted Mansion, but otherwise, it may be better to wait in the Standby line. A huge exception to this is during the holiday season, when the Mansion is transformed into the Haunted Mansion Holiday Nightmare. Lines are simply gigantic then, and using FASTPASS is a must.

At Tokyo DisneySea, Tower of Terror is where everyone goes first, though it will run out of FASTPASSES less rapidly than Monsters Inc or Pooh's Hunny Hunt. On crowded days, other attractions with long lines include Journey to the Center of the Earth, 20,000 Leagues Under the Sea, Indiana Jones Temple of the Crystal Skull, and the Magic Lamp Theater. Some folks may find the 3-D movie of the Magic Lamp Theater to be only mildly entertaining, but the attraction often sports a long wait that is better skipped by using FASTPASS.

Where to Use Standby

The non-holiday version of Haunted Mansion is a good candidate for Standby, as is MicroAdventure, a renamed Honey I Shrunk the Audience. All of these attractions will be highly familiar to park-goers who have visited either Disneyland or Walt Disney World. As a result, these attractions belong either on the list to skip entirely, or the list of attractions to visit using the Standby line. Keep those FASTPASS slots open for the big thrill rides!

Over in Tokyo DisneySea, Indiana Jones Adventure: Temple of the Crystal Skull belongs in the "Standby" category not because it has no crowds (it does), but because it, and the nearby Raging Spirits, features a single-rider line (more on this later) that you should use instead. As a result, there is no need to use up a valuable FASTPASS for either of these attractions.

FASTPASS is not needed at the Mermaid Lagoon Theater, as it is hidden deep inside the indoor kids area. This one, however, should not be skipped, as it is entertaining and innovative.

Obtaining a Second FASTPASS

When your FASTPASS ticket prints, you'll see not only a Return Time, but also a notice near its bottom that explains at what time you are eligible for another FASTPASS, either here or at another attraction. In general, you can only hold one FASTPASS at a time, but if the Return Time is far into the future, the system takes pity on you and allows you to obtain a second FASTPASS two hours after issuing the first. Thus, for a brief time, you might be holding two FASTPASSES, neither of which has yet reached its Return Time window.

This second ticket seems like a nice bonus, and thus something you might be tempted to consider merely optional, but remember, to really save time, you should not only use FASTPASS, but you must also fully maximize that usage. At the very moment your next window of time opens up to get another FASTPASS, send a runner out to the next attraction with all of your party's tickets. As a general rule, you should always hold as many FASTPASSES as you can until they run out for the day.

(No?) Late Return

Your FASTPASS ticket shows the date and Return Time window in bold font. You can't return early, and you can't use a FASTPASS ticket from a previous day (hence the boldface font indicating the date), but you can occasionally return a little bit late and still use it. Increasingly, however, visitors are denied entry for being late.

Be prepared for long lines in the middle of the afternoon, when all the FASTPASS tickets have been issued for the day. This is a time to ride smaller attractions, or simply to take a break.

One last idea about lines: in the United States, you can enter a line two minutes before the park closes, and thus "cheat" the operating hours a little bit. You will find some attractions closing early so that the line will be finished by the scheduled closing, so plan accordingly.

Where to Eat

Themed Restaurants

One of the defining features of the Tokyo Disney Resort experience is the high level of atmosphere and immersiveness in the park restaurants. A few isolated eateries are little more than outdoor snack stands, but the majority offer significant ambiance. If possible, visitors should eat at a wide variety of restaurants on the trip, or at least step inside each eatery, if for no other reason than to soak up the environment and the famous Disney theming.

The following is an abbreviated list of park restaurants, including only a select few that have a high level of theming. They are listed in (subjective) order, ranked by the quality of atmosphere. (Note: food quality is not a part of this ranking.)

Tokyo Disneyland

Pan Galactic Pizza Port – The animatronic Tony Solaroni makes a show upstairs of pretending to make pizza. A new event occurs every few minutes.

Queen of Hearts Banquet Hall – The themed kitchen is only the tip of the iceberg. Revel in the deeply themed mood lighting of the dining area.

Blue Bayou – Dine in the swamps of Louisiana, an atmosphere that is hard to beat.

Grandma Sara's Kitchen – Themed like below-the-surface warrens, the rooms of this eatery call to mind those critters which scurry under ground.

China Voyager – There are multiple outdoor dining areas to explore here, but most take up the themes of coastal and nautical exploration.

Tokyo DisneySea

Magellan's – The premier atmosphere at Tokyo DisneySea, Magellan's recalls the glory days of oceanic explorers, with a deeply detailed décor that screams refinement. The food is Western-style.

Vulcania Restaurant – A retreat carved into the rock of the volcano but embedded with metal here and there, Vulcania embodies the Jules Verne mythos and offers Chinese cuisine. Mysterious sound effects keep things interesting.

Yucatan Base Camp Grill – Music only adds to the rich theming that transports patrons to an ancient archeological ruin. The fare is Mexican in nature.

S.S. Columbia Dining Room – The height of luxury aboard an ocean liner, this dining room takes visitors to another era.

Sebastian's Calypso Kitchen – The undersea kingdom extends to this eatery and the little touches of oceanic life around its dining area.

Cape Cod Cook-Off – Cape Cod comes alive here, and not to be missed is a boat which self-destructs and reassembles.

Sailing Day Buffet – It's not a warehouse, it's the busy port terminal for transatlantic travel.

Sample Menu Items and Prices

Prices for food at Tokyo Disneyland and Tokyo DisneySea are surprisingly reasonable. Portions are smaller than American diners may be expecting, particularly when it comes to drink sizes, but the food is not automatically priced out of reach. Portions are smaller not only in Tokyo Disney parks, but throughout Japan, and indeed in most countries outside of America—the portions are, by nature, just not as large.

There are no disastrous eateries to steer entirely clear of, so in a way, everything is recommended, and you could really eat anywhere. What may matter more is your desire for a certain type of food, and the constraints of your budget.

At most restaurants with an indoor dining room, usually cafeteria (tray-slide) or table-service, you can find a water station and wax cups, so don't let the small sizes of the drinks ruin your meal. Just tank up on water instead.

It should be noted that, even at the full-service restaurants, the server may bring a bill, but patrons are expected to pay at the cashier on the way out, just as you might do at an American diner or coffee shop. The delivery of the bill to your table is not a signal that it's time to leave. Take as long as you'd like in the restaurant, and simply pay on your way out.

English Menus and Western Expectations

At most Tokyo Disney Resort restaurants, the menus are presented in both English and Japanese, sometimes in English first. However, you should be wary about ordering in English if you're using your normal pace of speech; the odds are good that the Cast Member might not understand you. Speaking slowly helps.

If a Cast Member does not offer it first, it may also be advisable to request an English menu, even if a sign overhead lists the words in English. You're likely to be handed a picture menu that makes it easy to point to the food items you want, something that is a lot harder to do if you're merely pointing at a sign full of words over the cashier's head.

To ask for a menu in English, say "ehgo no menyu wa … arimasu ka?" (literally: "English's menu…do you have it?") It will be helpful if you pause before the last part (arimasu ka), and speak slowly to increase the chance of being understood. And don't mutter—speak as clearly and distinctly as possible. The Japanese give equal weight to all syllables in a word, so avoid extra inflection.

Modern technology helps. If you decide what to order based on a dual-language menu outside the restaurant, snap a photo with your phone zoomed in on the item, including the

Japanese characters. You can show this photo to the cashier at the same time that you speak the words of your order.

If you are assembling your order from the menu out front, consider calculating the price at this early stage. Tax is included in the listed price, so you can have exact change ready before you even get into line.

Expect a stream of words in Japanese as the cashier hands you the receipt back; you're being told to show your ticket to the person at the counter. As a rule, cashiers are too polite to try to engage you in small talk.

Figuring out how to order is often the easy part. It is often harder to make the mental cultural switch to expect the right things in the restaurant and its menu choices. For instance, you won't find Diet Coke very often in the theme parks (in Japan, it's called "No Calorie Coca-Cola" when you can find it), presumably because obesity is not an epidemic and there is a correspondingly lower demand for it. You will find drinks that sound exotic, such as melon, lemon, grapefruit, or grape soda, or strawberry tea, and it's a good idea to experiment with all of them. You're visiting a foreign country, after all! Many of the drink choices are dictated by sponsorships. Don't expect to be able to order the same thing at every restaurant. Each eatery has its own set of drinks, and there is no consistency around the park as to what kind of drinks are served.

Speaking of drinks, you should know that some meals come complete with "soft drinks," but the term doesn't mean what you might expect. This does not refer to sodas, but rather to coffee, tea, or orange juice. In many restaurants, in fact, soda pop is not available at all.

You'll see references to "sets" on the menu, which is their version of a "combo meal." Typically, it includes a main item and a side dish. Some sets include drinks; others do not.

Do not assume that tray-slide and fast food restaurants offer a bevy of condiments somewhere in the dining area. There may be a few plastic utensils available, but the dizzying array of sauces and toppings seen in American eateries is likely to be entirely absent in Japan. You might, for instance, have to request ketchup from the cashier when you check out. Even salt and pepper are not normally on display.

Lastly, do not send the rest of your party to hold a table while you obtain the food. Usually your party will be asked to wait until the food is delivered to lock up a table, as space is often at a premium.

Food Carts

There are food carts sprinkled along the sides of almost every major walkway, selling items both familiar (popcorn, turkey legs) and unfamiliar (a hot dog-sized steamed gyoza dumpling). There are stands selling whole fruit as well, meaning you could make a whole meal out of items from vending carts. On busy days, though, even these carts sport long lines, sometimes impossibly long.

Of particular popularity are the flavored popcorn stands. Salted popcorn is in the minority here. Most popcorn sold has an unusual flavor or spice, and the two parks feature different varieties. These stands often generate enormous lines, especially the curry popcorn sold on the walkway between Westernland and Adventureland. At Tokyo Disneyland, you can buy varieties such as curry, honey, chocolate, caramel, and soda. At Tokyo DisneySea, varieties include strawberry, black pepper, cappuccino, chocolate, sea salt, and coconut.

Frequent visitors to Japan may wish to splurge on one of the souvenir popcorn buckets, which are eligible for refills at a reduced price, with no expiration date, so it can be used on future visits as well. The bucket is sturdy enough to endure several such trips.

Churros are another favorite snack, and are similarly available in different flavors. The cart near the Pirates of the Caribbean serves maple churros, while the cart in Tomorrowland serves honey-lemon churros. There's also black-sesame churros sold at the Arabian Coast.

In general, Japanese visitors tend not to walk while they are snacking on popcorn or other items from food carts. It is more common to find a seat somewhere, or to at least stand still, while eating. This isn't followed religiously, even by Japanese visitors, but foreign tourists may wish to adopt the custom nonetheless.

Tipping

Tipping is not expected or encouraged at any restaurants, even those offering table service. The price of the food item already takes into account the wages of the servers, so there is no need to feel guilty. If you try to leave a tip anyway, the Cast Member may chase after you, frantic that you seem to have accidentally left some of your money behind.

Reservations

Restaurant reservations aren't really a requirement in the non-holiday seasons, but they may be a good idea on the weekends. For the holiday seasons, and whenever school is out in Japan (not the same summer schedule as most American schools), then reservations become increasingly important for the table-service restaurants. At some prime locations, like the MiraCosta restaurants or the Blue Bayou, reservations are needed year-round and for every meal, including breakfast.

You are now able to make dining reservations online, and you can make them before your arrival if you already have reservations at a Disney hotel or an official hotel. To do so, simply call the official Tokyo Disney Resort Reservation Center, which open from mid-morning to mid-evening (local time). Dining reservations can be made one month in advance. Here is the number to call, with the most common international codes already attached:

United States:	011-81-45-683-3333
United Kingdom:	00-81-45-683-3333
Australia:	0011-81-45-683-3333

To determine other international codes, visit:
http://www.timeanddate.com/worldclock/dialing.html

However, you will not be able to make park dining reservations from your hotel, even from the Disney hotels. They can only handle reservations for their own hotel restaurants, where prices are often on the expensive side. The dinner shows absolutely require reservations.

A Typical Dining Transaction

Fast food purchases at Tokyo Disneyland and Tokyo DisneySea sometimes can create the most anxiety, since you cannot simply point at a pot of food like you do in a trayslide, nor can you point at a certain line in a menu like you do at a sit-down restaurant. So let's walk through the typical steps of such a transaction. Many of these will be applicable to a trayslide buffeteria or to a table-service meal as well.

1. The cashier will greet you with "Ohayo gozaimasu" in the morning, "Konnichiwa" in the late morning and daylight hours, and "Kombanwa" in the evening. You may feel free to repeat the greeting back.
2. You may try to ask for an English menu ("ehgo no menyu wa … arimasu ka?"), or you may try to order directly in English. Simplify as much as you can. If there is only one item containing chicken, then merely say "chicken" rather than the entire item name in English. If you took a picture of the menu item on your phone, show it now.
3. In Japanese, quantities are given after the noun. You will fit right in if you do the same, even though you are speaking English. ("Chicken, one.") It helps to raise

the correct number of fingers as you say the desired quantity.

4. Better yet, do the number part in Japanese. Learning numbers in Japanese requires knowing that there are multiple number systems: one for counting (as in money amounts), one for numbers of people, and one for quantities of generic things. For quantities, the numbers are hitotsu (one), futatsu (two), mittsu (three), and yottsu (four). Thus, our example becomes "Chicken, hitotsu." This numbering system goes up to ten, but if you need more than four of any item, you may wish to simply say it in English.

5. Almost always, your order will be read back to you, with the cashier often indicating quantities by holding up his or her own fingers.

6. You will then be read a large number, which is the amount of the bill (in yen). Don't panic if you don't recognize Japanese numbers verbally, since the digital numerals are always visible somewhere on the cash register. Often, the Cast Member will point at that readout while saying the numbers.

7. Look for a shallow tray the size of a large ashtray on the counter between the cashier and you. If one is there, it is meant for the money. Don't hand the money directly to the cashier unless this tray is absent. Instead, place the money onto the tray, where the cashier will scoop it out. Your change will be returned to you in the same fashion.

8. If you're paying by credit card, you may hear a question in Japanese. They are asking if it's okay with you to charge the card for the full amount in just one payment, rather than divide the meal(s) into multiple payment segments (this is often asked because JCB cards, common in Japan, allow for purchases to be spread out, with portions appearing on the monthly

bill for two or three months rather than the whole amount all at once). The cashier likely will raise a single finger and look questioningly at you while doing so. Reply "Hai" (yes) and raise a single finger to indicate it's okay to charge the card for a single purchase, rather than a spread-out purchase.

9. Credit cards are returned to you with the receipt wrapped around them. Usually you will not be asked to sign the receipt. Japanese clerks hand over an item using both hands and presenting it right-side-up so you can read it. You should receive the item using both of your hands, glancing down to verify that the amount is correct.

10. Your food will be delivered right away, with no need to step aside while another visitor is helped. You may sometimes be asked for your receipt before the food is served, so keep it out. You are likely to hear a parting wish for you to enjoy your meal; simply say "arigato gozaimasu" and head off to the dining area to find a table.

11. When you are done eating, you will fit in if you clear off your own table by throwing away the trash and stacking plates nearby. This is a common custom in Japan. That said, there are exceptions to this rule at Tokyo Disney theme parks, and you may find that a grateful Cast Member will hurry to take the tray from you as you head for the trash can. In table service restaurants, you never need to clear your own table.

If this description of a food purchase sounds daunting, take heart that Japanese workers are very forgiving of foreigners. They do not expect you to speak Japanese. It's actually quite easy to order in English if you need to, as long as you speak slowly and clearly. The rest will take care of itself!

Where to Shop

Where to Find What

Shopping at the Tokyo Disney Resort is always an interesting experience. You might think that the really big shop near the main entrance (Grand Emporium in Tokyo Disneyland, Emporio in Tokyo DisneySea) has everything, but that's not true. Nor is it true that the even larger shop outside Tokyo Disneyland (Bon Voyage) has everything.

It makes sense that items can be found somewhat close to the special rides and attractions. There's a lot of Tower of Terror merchandise, for instance, in the shop near the end of that ride. But sometimes you have to look slightly farther afield. Some of the Indiana Jones Adventure merchandise is across the river in Lost River Outfitters, near Miguel's El Dorado Cantina. And the Big Band Beat merchandise is housed all the way over at the Tower of Terror gift shop, as well as in McDuck's store nearby.

Even if stores with ideal locations near attractions do not have the merchandise you're looking for, it's possible that it is sold elsewhere. For instance, the shop in the middle of Mysterious Island should, you might think, sell all the merchandise for Journey to the Center of the Earth. However, the miniature attraction vehicles are not sold here, nor at either Emporio or Bon Voyage. We found them only at gift shops in the Disney hotels and the official hotels. The moral of the story is that you should poke your head into every store. You never know what delightful item might be in the next shop! Sometimes the merchandise located far afield is actually discontinued merchandise, with little inventory left. Product lines at the Tokyo Disney Resort often enjoy very short lifespans.

There's also a great variety of merchandise, especially if you consider the park as a whole. Unlike U.S. parks, which often stock the same items in multiple stores, the Japanese parks tend to offer completely different goods in each establishment, which makes shopping all the more fun.

Visitors may be surprised by the seemingly endless variety of cookies and crackers for sale in many of the stores. These items are hot sellers for Japanese tourists, since it is a common Japanese custom to bring back gifts of food for family members, friends, and coworkers when returning from a trip. Fight the temptation to just pass by the cookies. Many of them are packaged in decorative tins that are unique to particular attractions, and they make great souvenirs on their own.

Expect stores to be crowded at every moment of the day, except perhaps the very early morning. But that's also the time when you should be visiting attractions, so resign yourself to a crowded shopping experience. But don't wait for nightfall. As the evening progresses, stores become progressively more mobbed. It's a sight to behold, perhaps, but not an experience you'll want to live through by standing in line to make a purchase.

You'll find park-specific merchandise, especially keychains and commemorative plates that celebrate the current themed overlay of the park (such as Halloween, Christmas, or the A la Carte food festival). You may see a few ride-specific items, especially clothing. Don't expect tons of shirts or jackets branded with the park name, as this kind of item isn't very common. What is common is anything with Disney characters on it. You'll find a lot of items are branded to the characters rather than to the parks. The Japanese visitors have particular affection for some characters that might surprise you, like Duffy (Mickey's teddy bear), *Aladdin*'s Genie or Marie from *The Aristocats*. Moreover, you'll see lots of duplication of these kinds of items all over the park.

Bon Voyage

The largest store in Japan for Disney merchandise, Bon Voyage, sits between Tokyo Disneyland and the Maihama JR station. The two-story structure looks enormous from the outside, but the shop itself is only on the second floor, while the first floor is reserved for bathrooms and guest services, such as merchandise shipping. They ship internationally, but home delivery service is extraordinarily expensive if the destination is not within Japan. Be prepared to pack your own box. They don't handle a lot of international orders, so the language barrier may require tracking down a Cast Member who speaks English, while the right forms are hunted down. Shipping from your hotel may well be easier.

Bon Voyage duplicates many of the items for sale within the park, so don't expect an assortment of new merchandise you can't find elsewhere. Like the in-park stores, Bon Voyage dedicates a large percentage of floor space to cookies and snacks packaged in themed (usually character-based) containers.

Ikspiari

This shopping zone, situated next to Tokyo Disneyland, actually rests between the Ambassador Hotel and the park, so Western visitors might be forgiven for thinking of it as the local version of Downtown Disney. But the more apt comparison is to a typical shopping mall. Excepting one Disney Store in the middle, there's nothing particularly Disney about the architecture, theming, or design of this multi-level mall, which reverts to a basic brick pattern on the walls of the lowest floor. It was designed not by Walt Disney Imagineering, the usual wizards for park design, but by contractors of the Oriental Land Company, local owner of the Tokyo Disney Resort. Its name is a Japanese version of the word "experience."

Oddly, Ikspiari is not open in the early morning, so visitors staying at the Disney Ambassador Hotel must walk around the outside of Ikspiari to reach either the monorail station or the Maihama JR station. This is curious, since that captive audience would probably welcome a place to shop or eat in the early morning.

Most of the shops on the upper levels are upscale and will be familiar to Western shoppers. There are some tremendous restaurants in the upper floors, many of them justifiably famous. The bottom floor includes a parking garage, but the side facing the train station has several shops of interest, including a bookstore, a grocery store, and a highly affordable food court. The grocery store is an ideal place to find consumer staples you may have forgotten to pack, or to pick up drinks at a reasonable price. You might even find food you could prepare in your hotel room. The food court, open only later in the day and in the evening, offers an alternative to the overpriced Disney food, and with more authentic Japanese flavors. However, English-speaking employees are far less common here.

A Typical Shopping Transaction

Here's what to expect when you approach a cash register to pay for your items:

1. The cashier will greet you and will also likely thank you. If he doesn't extend his hands to take the items from you, place them on the counter.
2. Small talk is uncommon, so don't fret that you may be asked questions you can't answer.
3. If your purchases include electronic toys, the cashier will briefly turn on the toy to see that it is in working order.
4. After the cashier enters all of the items into the cash register, he will read the price to you and possibly point to the cash register display.
5. You may be asked if there is anything else. The way to say "that is all" is "sore de zenbu desu."
6. If paying with cash, look for a tray into which the money should be placed. If paying by credit card, hand the card directly to the clerk. In Japan, an item should be presented using two hands, with the item turned around so it is right-side-up for the receiver. You likely will not be asked to sign the receipt. After

the receipt prints out, it will be returned to you with your credit card. As described earlier, credit card payments sometimes result in the clerk asking whether you'd like the card charged "all at once" or to have the payment spread out over several months.

7. The cashier will individually wrap delicate or fragile items. Most items simply will be added to the large bag collectively. At Tokyo Disney parks the cashier also carefully folds up extra themed bags to stuff into the large bag. If you purchase four items, you'll get four Disney bags neatly folded up and placed into the large bag, providing you with an easy way to repackage items as gifts for friends.

8. During the bagging process, you may be asked a question in Japanese. If the item is one you might either give as a gift or want right away, the clerk is probably asking if you want the price tag removed. Even for toys or other gifts, a clerk may ask about the price stickers, in case you mean the items as gifts.

9. Alternately, you be asked about how to bag all the items. If you want to bag them together, just say so in English, or add the Japanese "issho ni."

10. The clerk will raise the bag to a vertical position and apply a piece of tape across the top, just below the plastic handles. That signifies everything in the bag has been paid for. Don't rip it open until you've left the store.

11. Lastly, the bag will be offered to you in a vertical position, held by the corners. Take the bag by the handles in the middle. The clerk may offer parting wishes. Simply reply "arigato gozaimasu" as you take the bag, and head off.

Hidden Treasures and Quiet Getaways

Tokyo Disneyland Hidden Treasures

In your rush to visit every attraction, don't go so fast that you forget to slow down and enjoy the beauty of the park around you. There are hidden details aplenty to capture your attention, help you relax, and further immerse you in the Disney experience.

For instance, watch for Indians all around the river, engaged in various activities.

The Snow White grotto is a lovely escape from the hubbub just moments away on the busy boulevard. Recreated from the Anaheim version (which was itself a gift from an Italian sculptor), this delightful display of Snow White, the dwarfs, and some cute animals, exists only to be seen and admired.

More interactive is the robot Tony Solaroni found in the Pan Galactic Pizza Port, near the exit to Star Tours. This restaurant has great pizza, but when you visit, make sure you eat upstairs to watch the never-ending robot show. Tony Solaroni operates a complex pizza-making device, and every few moments, some event occurs to distract him. There is also a running show on video monitors throughout the restaurant.

The entire apparatus exists only as additional, unnecessary theming, which makes discovering its existence all the more delightful. Nearby, an alien security guard will look familiar to Walt Disney World veterans, since his identical twin entertains visitors at a Tomorrowland restaurant in Orlando.

Watch for tributes in unexpected places. For instance, as the Western River Railroad passes by Big Thunder Mountain, a crate can be spotted nearby, addressed to "Dr. T. Baxter," as a tribute to Tony Baxter, the designer in Disney's famed Imagineering division who first created the Big Thunder Mountain concept.

Quieter areas in this theme park are hard to come by, but the extremities sometimes yield cul-de-sacs where little action is taking place. Portions of Tomorrowland nearest Toontown qualify as less-traveled, and quiet locales can be found on the water side of Big Thunder Mountain, or near the canoe loading dock alongside Splash Mountain. Another great quiet area can be found in the Indian camp behind the fort on Tom Sawyer Island.

Tokyo DisneySea Hidden Treasures

Great care was taken during the construction of Tokyo DisneySea to provide intricate detail, possibly the most ever in any theme park in the world. You could marvel for hours at the painted rocks, the twisted dead branches, and the steam fissures in Mysterious Island. The external walls of the MiraCosta are festooned with some windows that are real and functional, others that are merely painted, and still others that are half-and-half. (Authentic Italian painters were brought in to create the trompe l'oeil fake windows.) Speaking of the MiraCosta, don't forget to visit the lobby, where Hidden Mickeys are secreted in the ceiling panels, and perceptive image hunters might find Pinocchio dancing in the walls.

When you visit Mermaid Lagoon, take time to spot some of the many Hidden Mickeys embedded in the entrance walls. Deeper inside this land, don't assume the playground is just for kids; Ariel's treasure trove is in here, complete with a statue of Prince Eric as well as her knickknacks. And don't forget the toddler playground out in the main area of Mermaid Lagoon. Babies otherwise kept cooped up in strollers all day will appreciate this safe environment in which to stretch their legs.

A less-visited treasure is the fortress in the Mediterranean Harbor. There are maze-like corridors to run through, balconies and ramparts to visit, and hidden rooms inside which feature amazing theming. Printed quest-type games are handed out to provide a level of challenge to your explorations, but it's just as much fun to simply wander. Parts of the fortress and nearby docked ship are interactive. Tug on the cannons to watch them "fire" or pull the levels on some of the weird machines to see what happens.

Less-high profile attractions delight in simplicity, such as the Waterfront vehicles that never sport a line, yet transport your party around to enjoy the vistas from new angles.

The vehicles drop you off at Cape Cod, itself a hidden treasure. This sub-land of the Waterfront is less-traveled and all the more quaint and delightful for it. Keep an eye out also for Duffy, a Disney bear well-known to the Japanese but unknown to Western visitors. Before you leave the Waterfront, be sure to stop inside the S.S. Columbia. This full-sized ship houses two restaurants, but much of it is also available simply to wander through. Don't miss the breath-taking vistas of the park and nearby Tokyo Bay from atop the bow. On clear days, Mt. Fuji can be spotted from here.

Another attraction off the radar, yet delightful in its execution, is the Venetian Gondolas, which travel from canals near the hotel out into the harbor and back. Not to be missed is the fun of the Japanese skipper singing Italian opera!

Details hidden in plain sight, and with little obvious purpose other than to create atmosphere, provide some of the best moments of delight. A few prominent examples include the rotting aqueduct near Mysterious Island, the steaming manhole covers in the American Waterfront, and the jet of water gushing through a "leak" in the gates separating Port Discovery from Tokyo Bay. Watch the water in Port Discovery—those bubbles signify a submarine going by under water. And pay attention to the number on the plane that has "crashed" near the Indiana Jones Adventure to spot a connection with George Lucas!

If you're seeking quiet roads and areas, try either the area adjacent to the Indiana Jones Adventure or the Mexican-themed road opposite the river to the Indiana Jones Adventure, especially at night. After dark it's also quiet in much of the Arabian Coast.

Time Savers

FASTPASS

It's been covered at length previously, but FASTPASS is such a crucial component of a smooth vacation to the Tokyo Disney Resort that it must be stressed again. Use FASTPASS early, use it often, and you'll save time. Choose not to use FASTPASS, and you'll not only fail to save time, your wait times will actually increase (you will LOSE time), because so many other people are using FASTPASS. Their gain is your loss, translated into longer Standby lines. Without using FASTPASS, you might only see four attractions per day.

Single Rider Lines

Tokyo Disneyland doesn't have any rides which offer a service for single riders, but Tokyo DisneySea has three of them: 20,000 Leagues Under the Sea, the Indiana Jones Adventure, and Raging Spirits. At 20,000 Leagues Under the Sea, part of the fun is being in an enclosed space with the rest of your party and exchanging squeals of delight at what you're seeing, so it's advisable to use either FASTPASS or Standby lines for this particular attraction.

At the Indiana Jones Adventure and Raging Spirits, you may want to use the single rider line, rather than the Standby line. Although both offer FASTPASS, the presence of the single rider line at these attractions argues for keeping your FASTPASS slots open for other rides. It does mean you will not ride on the same vehicle as other people in your party, but this is a small price to pay for saving a huge amount of time (often an hour or more). The ride experience here doesn't lend itself to sharing or talking while you are on the ride, like the way it does at 20,000 Leagues Under the Sea. The experience while alone is all but identical.

At Raging Spirits, approach a Cast Member at the attraction's entrance and let him or her know your desire to find the single rider line. If you wish to use Japanese, simply hold up your index finger and proclaim "hitori nori," which the Cast Member will likely repeat, and also add "single rider" in English for good measure. You will be escorted to a special line which leads right up to the loading platform. It's unlikely there will be anyone in the single rider line ahead of you. As soon as a party appears with an odd number of members, you'll be called forward to join their row. In my experience, this takes less than a minute most of the time. A minor delay is not uncommon.

Things work a bit differently at the Indiana Jones Adventure, where the single rider line doesn't begin at the attraction entrance. Instead, you step into the Standby line, and almost right away, as you round a corner, you'll see a small sign and gate leading off to a new path for single riders. (Note: late in the evening, this will be closed because the Standby line is so short; just use it instead.) If the Standby line is so full that you'd have to wait in switchbacks prior to this turnoff, ask a Cast Member for assistance. Single rider service at the Indiana Jones Adventure is offered only on busy days.

Once in the single rider line, you'll have your own pathway through the temple queue. When you reach the merge point of the FASTPASS and Standby queues, the Cast Member will verify that you are a single rider and escort you forward to the room with the safety spiels. There, As visitors stream past, the Cast Member will identify a group with three members and interrupt the line for you to insert yourself. It often happens wordlessly, or, at most, an explanation is given to the party following you as to why you were allowed to cut into the line. From there, proceed through the line as usual. When asked at the platform how many are in your party, hold up your index finger and say "hitori."

If you decide to use "single rider" at 20,000 Leagues Under the Sea, inquire at the front of the attraction as to what you must do to access this feature.

Child Switch

Though it's unadvertised, there is a child switch service for parties traveling with youngsters who cannot ride with them. In such parties, an adult would normally be forced to experience the thrill ride alone while the other adult watches the child off the ride. But that would mean the second adult also has to wait in line, effectively punishing the party for having children or elderly members who cannot ride with them.

The "alternating rider" system fixes this problem. Before getting in line, inquire at the front of the attraction about the need to switch riders. The second adult will be given a card while the first one waits in line (or uses the FASTPASS Return line, if holding a valid FASTPASS). When the first adult returns after the ride, the second adult can ride without delay. Unlike American parks, where the second adult is told to join the FASTPASS line, the second adult is escorted through the exit or a backdoor entrance right up to the loading platform and given priority treatment. This way, a minimum of time is lost.

Best of all, the alternating rider system does not "punish" parties for using FASTPASS, as long as both adults hold a valid FASTPASS. If you have

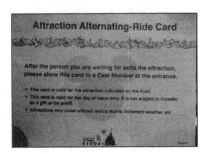

FASTPASSES, you could simply take turns waiting in the Return queue, but you'd lose time. Using the rider switch system, you don't lose time. At the right return time, both adults let the attraction Cast Member know of their intention, and the first adult joins the line normally. The second adult surrenders his FASTPASS for a rider switch card and thus bypasses even the nominal queue in the FASTPASS return line.

Amazingly, the backdoor service can also be used in conjunction with "single rider." As usual, announce your

desire at the main entrance, join the single rider line, and when the first rider is done, the second adult will be escorted directly to the platform. This is one highly friendly system for families!

The rider switch card is called "koutai riyou kaado" (koh-tie dee-yoh card-oh) in Japanese. The full phrase to inquire about using this service would be: "Koutai riyou kaado… arimasu ka?"

Restaurant Hints

Especially during peak periods and on weekends, the restaurants become quite busy and feature long lines during lunch and dinner hours. On such days, you'll save a maximum amount of time by eating when no one else is, doing so either before the lunch rush or between lunch and dinner. Make do with snacks instead.

As a general rule, it's better to eat lunch early than to wait until after the lunch rush, since lines are still fairly long in the afternoon. To really save time, grab an early breakfast, eat lunch as soon as restaurants open at 10:30 or 11:00 (stuffing yourself silly), and then don't eat again until after you leave the park in the evening. That might mean stopping for a snack at a food cart, if you're staying long. Carts get long lines during meal hours too, so one effective strategy is to visit carts early, buy items that will keep (like whole fruit or bags of chips), and store them in your backpack or purse until later in the day. You could also bring in outside food for this same purpose, purchased early in the morning from the convenience store at Maihama JR station. However, bringing outside food into the park is technically not allowed, and it occurs in Tokyo Disney Resort parks less often than in the American parks.

Money Savers

Coupons or Discounts

Because Tokyo Disneyland and Tokyo DisneySea are in such high demand, there are no discounts on park admission.

In a way, though, the multi-day passes provide discounts. As you might expect, the longer you stay, the less you pay per day. Of course, this strategy comes with longer and more expensive hotel bills, so you might wish to minimize expenses by switching to a lower-cost hotel. If you're staying at a regular Disney hotel, for instance, consider moving all of your nights to an official hotel such as the Hilton or Sheraton, which often costs only half as much. If you're determined to experience the Disney magic at Disney hotels, consider staying there one night and then moving to an official hotel for ensuing nights. The monorail makes switching hotels easy and convenient.

You won't find any food coupons, either. The only way to save money on food is to eat less of it, or eat the cheaper items (or both). These ideas are explored below.

There are no discounts for the Disney hotels. They are always fully booked and have no need to offer discounts. However, those seeking to pinch pennies need not despair. The official hotels are competitively, even reasonably, priced and offer almost the same conveniences as the Disney hotels (the Ambassador Hotel, in particular, suffers by comparison). Even cheaper are hotels located off-property, either in the vicinity or in downtown Tokyo. The JR rail system makes it easy to access the TDR resort on each day you wish to visit, though trains are sometimes crowded early in the morning, particularly on work days.

Skipping the Monorail

It costs a few dollars to use the Resort Line for each one-way trip, or about $9 for an all-day pass. A simple way to save money is to take your hotel's free shuttle to the park rather than the monorail, though that method is less convenient, may take longer, and will be more crowded. Also, strollers will have to be folded. Additionally, the official hotels only run shuttles to the monorail, not the parks directly, on the less crowded days. Walking to the park is really only possible if your hotel is directly in front of the park entrance (or if you're at the Ambassador). Any other hotel-to-park walk will take far longer than you're hoping. At that point, it's probably worth it to pay for the monorail.

Restaurant Strategies

At the restaurant, one certain way to save money is to skip the drinks. Fast food locations usually don't have water stations, but drinking fountains will be located nearby. At tray slides and bigger fast food locations that have their own dining rooms, look around for a water station that will be stocked with cups and completely free of charge.

A tried-and-true method to reduce costs is to split meals between two people. In Japan, portions are smaller than in America, so don't count on this strategy to work every time.

Still, it may be enough to split a bowl of noodles or a large plate consisting of an entrée plus sides.

Child meals are available for a smaller price, though, of course, the portions are smaller. They are supposed to be available only for children, though you will not be asked to produce your child as proof.

The remaining advice boils down to good common sense. Skip dessert, which is often the highest-margin profit item for the restaurant, and thus costs much more than a budget-minded person wants to pay. Appetizers are in the same boat. Stick to main courses, splitting them with other people when possible. Of course, don't overdo it, either. You paid a lot of money to get here (just think of the airfare and hotel costs), so saving a few dimes may not be as high a priority as creating a memorable experience.

Food Carts

If you're looking to save time in the parks and avoid restaurants, you may wish to use the food carts to find occasional snacks. Perhaps the best source for these are carts selling whole fruit, like bananas and apples, for very reasonable prices. These carts are noted on the official guide map, including the map available in English.

By thinking creatively and busting your diet, you can allow these snacks to replace meals. A warm pretzel, for instance, can replace a whole meal for a child, even though those for sale here are smaller than those in other Disney parks. Or you could opt for the turkey leg, which is cheaper than the Disney World version, but is only half the size.

These food carts take only cash, not credit cards. Be sure to either take some cash into the park with you, or plan on visiting the ATM inside the park.

Snacks From Outside

Probably one of the most realistic strategies for saving money is to bring snacks with you into the park. While there is a brief bag check outside the main entrance, you will not be stopped for bringing some fruit or small snacks with you into the park. (Trying to bring a whole cooler or roller bag might be another matter.) As noted previously, bringing in outside food is technically not allowed, but if you are not obvious about it, you likely will not be harassed. Lockers outside the parks can accommodate baggage not allowed inside the parks.

Theoretically, you could bring snacks all the way from your home into Japan (not fruit, which is forbidden), but why waste the luggage space? Buy snacks at the grocery store at the bottom floor of Ikspiari. Do this the night before, as Ikspiari won't be open early in the morning when you head to the parks. What will be open is Newdays, a convenience store at the Maihama JR station, quite near the Welcome Center. In fact, it will be crowded, though the lines move quickly. Inside, you'll find candy, chips, cookies, bottled drinks and sodas, prepackaged sandwiches (some without crusts), and triangles of rice wrapped with seaweed. Commonly called onigiri (rice balls), these tasty snacks are hyper-affordable and feature a filling in the center like cooked tuna or kelp, as indicated by the different colors on the wrappers. Larger pre-made "lunch boxes" called bento also can be purchased here.

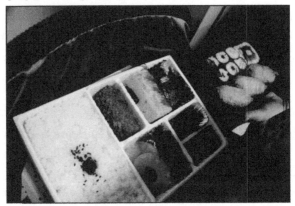

Stock up at Newdays before your entry into the park, and you'll save a lot of money. If nothing else, drinks here are affordable and easy. A caveat: if you are buying one-way tickets to use the monorail, your stop at the Resort Gateway Station (where the JR station is located) means you'll either have to walk from this point onward, or buy another monorail ticket. If you've got a multi-day monorail ticket, though, it functions as an all-day pass, to be used as often as you wish.

Eat Outside the Park

One use of your snacks from Newdays could be to eat right away, perhaps in line at the main entrance, before the park opens. In fact, you may spot Japanese visitors doing the same thing.

Your other choice for breakfast is Becker's, a little coffee shop next to Newdays (it becomes a burger joint for lunch and dinner). The menu includes breakfast croissant sandwiches of several varieties, and some interesting flavor combinations like chicken pesto on a croissant. The breakfast here is fresh and hot, and it is certainly more affordable than the Disney restaurants, but not as cheap as items from the convenience store. Those sensitive to smoke should note that half of the seating inside the cafe is for smokers, which really means the entire airspace fills with smoke.

Open as early as 7:00 is a restaurant in Ikspiari called It's Mono Café, though prices here are not as cheap as they are at the croissant shop.

You may be able to glimpse a noodle shop inside the JR train station, but you can't go in there to buy food unless you hold either a valid JR ticket or a JR Pass that was already activated either at the airport or Tokyo Station.

Among the cheapest of all options is to visit the grocery store and buy food that can be prepared in your hotel room, such as ramen and noodle bowls. You'll usually be offered chopsticks when you buy the noodle bowls. All you'll need is hot water, which is easy to obtain in your hotel room. In addition to a coffee maker (simply click to make coffee but don't add coffee grounds), you are likely to find a hot water heater for tea packets. The water will be hot enough for your noodle bowls, and you can eat in your hotel room and save quite a bit of both time and money. The very skittish may even wish to bring along ramen and cup-of-noodles from their home countries in a second suitcase, eating in the hotel room constantly and using that now-free suitcase space for souvenirs.

A great option for saving money is to avoid eating dinner in the parks. Instead, make your way to Ikspiari after you leave the park. The full-service restaurants here are not quite as expensive as the park restaurants, but the real savings can be found downstairs in the food court. The ramen and udon shop, in particular, has tremendous prices and authentic flavors, and meals cost about half what they would cost inside the park.

Those seeking a more familiar experience can find standard restaurants inside Ikspiari, including a Rainforest Café. However, the prices here are not particularly affordable.

Visitors may want to think twice about skipping the Disney restaurants inside the park. While it is possible to save money by bringing food into the park, or by leaving the park to eat, the overall experience of the day may be diminished somewhat. Each visitor will have to decide for himself or herself if the savings are really worthwhile.

Cheap Souvenirs

You will want mementos from your trip to Tokyo Disneyland and Tokyo DisneySea, but if you find the prices too high for the items you want, just look for less expensive souvenirs. On-ride photos are cheaper at Tokyo Disneyland and Tokyo DisneySea than at American parks, even though they are not inexpensive. Cheap souvenirs can be found in the form of ride vehicle miniatures, pens, stickers, buttons, mini-plush, magnets, and keychains customized to the resort or to specific attractions. Don't buy items that just have characters on them. These can be purchased in the United States far more cheaply. An exception would be characters who are hard to find stateside, such as Marie the cat.

Perhaps the best solution of all is to compile a collection of free items that are given away in the theme park, but work like souvenirs for you, once you get home. Ephemera such as cups, bibs, and guide maps can be placed into a scrapbook, giving character to otherwise plain pages.

Speaking of maps, be sure to pick up not just the English translations, but the Japanese versions as well. They are more colorful and just as effective for scrapbooking.

Don't forget about photos with characters and live performers, which provide personalized keepsakes that cost you nothing, except perhaps printing costs.

A final idea is to keep unused FASTPASS tickets for this purpose. You might go so far as to collect FASTPASSES for late at night when you don't plan to use them, knowing you'll instead keep them as free souvenirs.

Visiting With Babies, Toddlers, or Preschoolers

Surviving the Long Plane Ride and Jet Lag

If your child is a baby, and you're considering saving money by letting your child sit on your lap all the way to Japan, you should know that many airlines handle this option differently on international flights (as opposed to domestic flights). You might be assessed a fuel surcharge of several hundred dollars. If the surcharge is large enough, and the cost for a child's ticket is low enough, you may decide it's worth it to just buy the ticket. Indeed, the extra space makes the long flight (11-plus hours from Los Angeles, fourteen if traveling from the East coast) much more tolerable. Without it, you may find yourself greatly strapped for space. Note that according to FAA rules, children over two years of age cannot occupy a lap when flying.

For children who are required by law to use car seats or boosters when riding in a car, there is no such requirement for an airplane. You are free to consider a child as a lap infant if you can make do without the extra seat. If your child does have an individual seat, no booster or car seat is required (in fact, booster seats can not be used under FAA rules). This is fortunate, because you will not need a car seat in Japan, unless you plan to rent a car. This gives you one less bulky thing to lug around. The trains and buses have no car seat requirement, and although such a seat is technically required for riding in taxis, the driver is unlikely to turn you away. Whether you want to risk your child's safety in that fashion, of course, is a decision only you can make.

One final word about infants: you can take a small amount of liquid formula with you onto the airplane—it's one of the excused substances on the TSA's item-restriction list. But it's simpler to use powdered formula, mixing it with water as needed. For this, you can buy bottled water in the airport terminal after you've cleared security, or get water from flight attendants. The latter is a great option if you need hot or warm water. One effective strategy is to request hot water before the flight leaves the gate. It will cool before you need it, and be comfortably warm later on.

The above-mentioned "need" for formula at the proper temperature refers not to your baby's eating habits, but to the changing pressure in the airplane cabin during take-off and descent. Adults know to yawn, but children who do not understand this need to be coaxed to pop their ears every so often. The primary way to accomplish this is to get them to eat or drink, thus swallowing in the process, which can relieve pressure on their ears. It is very important that you start the feeding session early (before the pressure has built up to painful levels), because there is no calming down a child after a certain point. If the baby is eating solids, tiny crackers are an ideal complement to a bottle because the chewing helps, and you can delay each bite until the baby opens wide, mimicking a yawn and relieving pressure. Of course, don't start feeding so early that the baby is full before the plane finishes its initial ascent or major descent. Timing is everything.

For babies as well as older children, a primary challenge is how to entertain them during the long plane ride. If naps are possible, choose a flight time that makes it likely your child will sleep. Infants under one year of age may be small enough to use an in-plane bassinet. These are usually found only in the bulkhead seats near the front of a section. If you're interested in access to such a convenience, arrange to use those seats when you book the flight, check with a gate agent before boarding, or check with a flight attendant once you board the plane to see if a switch in seats is possible. Infants sleeping in bassinets make for happy parents (and fellow passengers) on an airplane. On most airlines, a baby must fit completely in the bassinet, cannot be able to sit up independently, and can't weigh more than 25 pounds.

But the children need to be entertained. Very young kids are unlikely to watch an entire movie with you on the screen in the airplane, though you may have better luck with a portable DVD player that you bring with you, along with favorite movies (remember that airline policies require the use of headsets for DVD players). Make a massive list of games, activity books, toys, and electronic games to bring with you, including at least fifteen items. Remember, you've got to survive not one, but two, very long plane rides. One effective strategy is to buy toys specifically for the plane, so the toys are brand new to your child and interest in them will last longer.

Lastly, be conscious of jet lag. The time difference from Los Angeles to Tokyo is 16 or 17 hours (depending on daylight savings). This may feel like a seven-hour time difference if you think of Tokyo being a complete day ahead (when it's 2:00 p.m. in LA, it's 7:00 a.m. and the next day in Tokyo). For children used to East coast time, the 14-hour time difference is even more jarring. Night and day are completely reversed. If your child is in a stroller, you might consider not making any special changes. Just go about your business normally, knowing the child will sleep in the stroller when necessary. During the night, though, expect to be awakened by the child, who is probably quite perplexed that it's dark outside despite feeling fully rested. If possible, parents should take turns being responsible for children needing acclimation; this way, at least one parent is well-rested each day, and no one becomes sleep-deprived while helping the family make the transition. Some travelers use a non-prescription (and non-addictive) antihistamine like Benedryl to induce drowsiness artificially on the plane or in the hotel room.

Baby Centers

Both Tokyo Disneyland and Tokyo DisneySea have baby care centers with multiple services for infants. Here you'll find plentiful changing tables, highchairs for feeding, private rooms for mothers to use for nursing, a kitchen for cleaning bottles or preparing food, and restrooms for small kids. These services are all free. You'll also find a small store selling formula, baby snacks, diapers, wipes, and just about anything else you'll need, all for surprisingly reasonable prices.

Nursing publicly in Japan is less common than in the United States, though it's not entirely unheard of. Most Japanese visitors are more inclined to visit the Baby Center than to nurse in public, even if they have a blanket for covering up. If you do nurse in public, either with or without a blanket drawn over you, you will not be disturbed, and you won't draw undue attention, either. It's just that the Japanese themselves tend to do it less often.

The Baby Center at Tokyo Disneyland can be found at the rear of Toontown, next to Roger Rabbit's Car Toon Spin, and there's another between World Bazaar and Tomorrowland. At Tokyo DisneySea, the Baby Center is at the front of the park, between the entrance to the MiraCosta and Café Portofino.

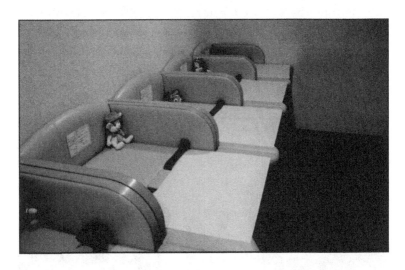

Changing Tables

Just like their American counterparts, the parks in Tokyo feature changing tables in all of the women's restrooms. However, the vast majority of men's restrooms do not have changing tables, not even the pull-down Koala-style plastic variety. One restroom in Tokyo Disneyland that does feature changing tables in the men's room can be found where Tomorrowland meets World Bazaar, near the Toy Station store. At Tokyo DisneySea, the bathroom in the corner of the

American Waterfront, near Tower of Terror, has a changing table which is accessible to men.

Strollers

Sturdy metal strollers are available to rent at Tokyo Disneyland and Tokyo DisneySea, but you will probably want your own stroller, just to save money, maximize comfort, and make travel easier through airports, train stations, and hotels. If you do bring your own stroller, do not plan to bring a massive all-in-one system that eats up a lot of space. That may not be out of place at Walt Disney World, but it definitely would be the largest stroller in Tokyo Disneyland. Opt for a lighter, smaller stroller, either the "umbrella" variety or just one that folds up small. Gate-check it just before you board your plane, and you'll have it back as soon as you disembark in Tokyo.

On one hand, the parks are quite stroller-friendly. You can roll the stroller, with the child still in it, right onto the monorail or the steamer transit ride at Tokyo DisneySea. On the other hand, though, you'll have to fold the stroller to use the resort shuttle buses at the beginning and end of the day. And Tokyo DisneySea features something Tokyo Disneyland lacks: long switchbacks that cut through staircases. That may make the inclines capable of handling wheelchairs and strollers, but these switchbacks take longer to navigate than

the stairs. You'll find switchbacks at these locations: the aqueduct, the boat next to the fortress, the exit to Mermaid Lagoon, the entrance to the Lost Delta, and the exit to the Arabian Coast.

On the plus side, any child in a stroller is likely to be greeted by passing Cast Members and offered a character sticker. In fact, over the course of your vacation, you may get showered with so many stickers, you'll be tempted to start a collection for your scrapbook back home. It's likely you'll be offered enough to complete the collection!

Buying More Supplies

While the Baby Centers do stock some additional supplies, you'll find a larger variety at the grocery store in Ikspiari, on the bottom level. The grocery store is also a much better place to buy additional baby food. If you'd rather have familiar flavors on hand for your baby, consider bringing along a supply from home that is large enough to last your entire vacation. Everything else—snacks, diapers, wipes, formula— can be found at the grocery store. The format of the baby formula may surprise you. Portions are packaged into individual paper tubes. Simply rip open one tube for each four ounces of formula you wish to mix.

Diapers, if you need them, are sold according to the weight of the baby in kilograms. (Just remember that a kilo is equal to 2.2 pounds, and you should be all right.) We've heard anecdotal (though conflicting) evidence that diapers bought in Japan, even brands you've seen in America, are less absorbent.

Child Switch

As mentioned in the chapter on "Time Savers," parents can avoid having to stand in line twice by using rider-switch passes. They are available for the asking at the entrance to many attractions.

No Lap Infants on Rides

In the U.S. Disney parks, infants are allowed to ride with parents by sitting on their laps. This is not allowed at Tokyo Disneyland and  Tokyo DisneySea, even on favorites that you may have experienced in America, such as Pirates of the Caribbean, It's a Small World, the dark rides, or the steam trains. The same rule applies to Pooh's Hunny Hunt. To ride these attractions, children must be able to sit by themselves. If they lack that ability, parents will have to experience the ride using the child-switch option.

Toddler Playground

A soft-padded, vinyl-covered play area in Mermaid Lagoon gives toddlers and infants a place to relax and stretch out. Older children will be asked to remain outside the play zone, since they sometimes jump around too vigorously and endanger smaller kids. Parents are welcome to come in to supervise their youngsters, but everyone entering the area must remove their shoes.

Height Requirements for Thrill Rides

Preschoolers will find they are welcome on most rides with no height requirement, which even includes rides with mild thrills like 20,000 Leagues Under the Sea, Pirates of the Caribbean, and Pooh's Hunny Hunt. The aforementioned requirement to be able to sit unaided will still be enforced, however.

Some rides do have minimum height requirements:

Tokyo Disneyland
- Splash Mountain: 90 cm (35 inches)
- Space Mountain: 102 cm (40 inches)
- Star Tours: 102 cm (40 inches)
- Big Thunder Mountain Railroad: 102 cm (40 inches)
- Gadget's Go Coaster: 90 cm (35 inches)

Tokyo DisneySea
- Tower of Terror: 102 cm (40 inches), and 3 yrs old
- Journey to the Center of the Earth: 117 cm (46 inches)

- Indiana Jones Adventure: 117 cm (46 inches)
- Raging Spirits: 117 cm (46 inches). This ride also has a maximum height of 195 cm (6 feet, 4 inches)
- Flounder's Flying Fish: 90 cm (35 inches)

Child Parade Viewing Areas

Some parades offer child-specific zones, which can be a lifesaver for kids who would otherwise struggle to see over the crowds. In some cases, parents are allowed to sit with their children here, but to be left here unattended, children will be need to be of elementary school age. Check with a park attendant when you arrive at the parade area.

Some Japanese Words You Should Learn

Won't English Be Enough?

If you want a quick answer, then yes, English may be enough. For simple situations, that is. But don't expect that everyone around you will speak perfect English. You may have heard that most Japanese citizens speak English, or at least understand it. It may be true that they've studied it in school, but many are not as comfortable speaking English as they are listening to it, so you are best served learning a little Japanese. Besides, it's inconsiderate to show up in a country without at least making a decent effort to learn and speak some of the language.

Even in the well-visited Disney parks in Tokyo, the Cast Members don't speak perfect English. You will find some excellent English skills at the front desk of most hotels, but the same level of skill doesn't necessarily extend to the entire hotel staff. Attractions Cast Members are probably next best at speaking English, followed by merchandise workers. Workers in restaurants and custodial workers are least likely to speak fluent English.

Signs almost always use both languages, but overhead announcements, safety warnings, and live spiels (if not pre-recorded) are likely to be delivered only in Japanese. Some announcements, including parade reminders and most safety spiels, are given in both languages. Expect rides and shows to be presented only in Japanese, from the Jungle Cruise and Country Bear Jamboree, to 20,000 Leagues Under the Sea and

Aladdin's Magic Lamp Theater. Helping matters somewhat, Aladdin's Theater offers a nifty handheld device which displays an English translation, perfectly timed with the show. A short cartoon panel on a small piece of a paper at Sindbad's Storybook Voyage provides some of the lyrics and storyline for the attraction in English.

Although you may not hear much English, you'll probably be able to cope without it. The Cast Members manage to talk amazingly well with their hands. When telling you where to stand at an attraction, they will hold up the proper number of fingers to indicate which line to stand in. Frequently, they will also escort you all the way there, gesturing with open palms, and the meaning is quite plain, even if you don't understand a word of Japanese.

Expect a two-handed gesture when the row is a number higher than five. Row eight, for example, may be her palm held up vertically with all fingers extended (this part means "five"), and also three fingers from the other hand held against it (because five plus three equals eight). She will also say the

number of the row in Japanese (scroll down for basic
Japanese), plus the word for row ("bahn-go").

A typical interaction might look like this:

- Cast Member: Nan Mest? ("how many")
- Me: Yon-Nin ("four people"), holding up
  four fingers
- Cast Member: Bahn-go Roku ("row six"), holding up
  five fingers on one hand, plus one
  finger of the other hand, held against
  the first five.
- Me: Hai, Bahn-go Roku (confirming "yes,
  row six", usually while nodding).

Or, just do the whole thing in English. You'll be fine. I prefer
to be the courteous tourist when possible, speaking the
language they do, but you really can make do with just
English (and hand gestures!) if needed.

If you're carrying a camera, expect a stream of words and a
universal gesture for "forbidden" (they'll cross their forearms
in an X, or perhaps just their palms). Almost always, they
don't mean that flash pictures are forbidden. They mean that
all pictures are disallowed, which is frequently the case in
Tokyo Disney Resort attractions.

The further you stray from the theme parks, the more likely
you will be spoken to in Japanese, and people will not be able
to understand your English. Don't assume that taxi drivers
(even in large cities like Kyoto) will understand English—
there just aren't that many Western visitors. As a general rule,
most Japanese can read English better than they can speak it.

Phrase Book or Dictionary

It may seem cliché to imagine yourself flipping through a phrase book for the right words while a clerk or attendant waits patiently, but sometimes this is your only option. A small dictionary may help with individual words, but most non-Japanese speakers are better served with a phrase book that is organized around certain scenarios and encounters, and which provides the most common phrases you can expect to need. The best and least expensive such phrase book is *Just Enough Japanese*, which can be purchased at most bookstores, or online.

You'll want to commit several key phrases to memory before your trip begins, just to avoid those awkward pauses while you thumb through a book. It may also help to consult your phrase book before entering an imminent transaction, if you have the time to spare. (Be considerate time-wise if there is a long line of customers waiting behind you.) Many commonly-used phrases are included in the following sections.

Learning Some Japanese Before Your Trip

It will reinforce your learning of key phrases if you approach the problem from multiple angles. Repetition helps, too. You'll get much further if you branch out beyond phrase books and use some auditory tools, too.

Ideally, this should take the form of a set of compact discs crafted to teach you the language just by you listening and repeating phrases. These sets are often sold with accompanying workbooks or handbooks, which can also help your study of the language. But don't feel compelled to dive into the written materials any more deeply than your natural inclination suggests. It will still be useful if you just listen to the CDs during your commute to work. But you must listen in an active sense. It won't work to let your mind wander while the Japanese phrases drone on in the background. This takes some getting used to, but it's worth it.

One CD learning set that provides a good mixture of pronunciation, vocabulary, and grammar is "Instant Immersion: Japanese Audio Deluxe." If the purchase price is too steep for your needs, see whether your local public library carries it.

If you do purchase a CD set, do not worry too much about scenarios and situations that are unlikely to arise on your tourist-oriented vacation. If you don't need to focus on talking about families or meeting business associates, just skip forward to how to order food in restaurants.

For those who don't wish to invest as much time as a CD set normally requires, there may be another option. Some public libraries subscribe to Rosetta Stone, an interactive click-and-talk program viewable through your Web browser. The repetition will help your vocabulary skills, but the real benefit here is pronunciation. If you don't hear and actively practice proper pronunciation, your Japanese is unlikely to be understood by most Cast Members once you arrive at the Tokyo Disney Resort.

No matter how you pursue pronunciation practice, make sure you do it actively. Mere listening is not as effective as opening your mouth and forming the words audibly. And forget just playing the words as background noise while your attention is elsewhere. Language abilities simply cannot be acquired via osmosis. The new vocabulary and pronunciation cannot just penetrate your skin by virtue of being in your presence. You must work at this, and at times it will feel like work. But take heart in knowing that the rewards will be great. Note also that, no matter how good your pronunciation is, some Japanese Cast Members may be amused at hearing a Westerner speak Japanese. Don't be offended. They are just not used to hearing Westerners speaking their language. In a way, this is a compliment to your efforts.

Initial Details About Japanese Grammar

As a tourist, you won't need to learn a lot of complex grammar rules. However, the phrase books will make a lot more sense, and you can almost translate word-for-word, if you keep in mind a few facets of Japanese grammar that are different from English grammar:

Word Order

A typical Japanese sentence assumes that the subject of the sentence is obvious and leaves it implied. The sentence often will begin with the object of the sentence, or perhaps an adjective. The verb comes last. Here are some samples:

English grammar: "I'm going to the arcade."
Japanese grammar: "Arcade towards go."
Japanese: "Game-Center ni ikimasu"

English grammar: "I don't speak Japanese."
Japanese grammar: "Japanese don't speak."
Japanese: "Nihon-go wa dekimasen."

Implied First-Person

As can be seen from the examples above, it's usually not necessary to say the word "I" in a declarative sentence. It's merely understood to be the implied subject of the sentence. One major exception comes when announcing your name:

English grammar: "I am John Smith."
Japanese grammar: "I Smith, John am."
Japanese: "Watashi wa Smith, John desu."

Verb Conjugation

As a tourist on a quick visit, you won't need to formulate complex sentences or talk about people other than yourself. Grant yourself the freedom to forget about verb conjugations except for first-person usage.

Desu

"Desu" is the conjugated verb for "to be"; it means either "I am" or "s/he is."

> English grammar: "This is delicious."
> Japanese grammar: "delicious is."
> Japanese: "Oishii desu."

> English grammar: "I am from Florida."
> Japanese grammar: "Florida from am."
> Japanese: "Florida kara desu."

You'll also encounter "desu" in one other way that might confuse you. Japanese use set phrases and inject them into sentences with frequency. One such phrase is "ii desu ne" (pronounced "ee des nay") that literally means "that's good, right?" Many sentences end with "ii desu ne" as a way of formally ending a thought.

Silent Letters

The most visible silent letter in Japanese (when written with the same alphabet used for English) is the final "u" in verb conjugations: desu, tabemasu, kimasu. These are pronounced as if there is no "u" present: des, tah-bay-mas, kee-mas.

A second instance occurs when a "u" appears in the middle of "suk"; the "u" becomes "swallowed" so far that it is practically inaudible. Examples: sukoshi (sko-shi), musuko (moose-ko)

Noun Markers

In many sentences, nouns are set off from the rest of the sentence via a special word, a marker whose meaning amounts to "everything before this is the noun." The two most common markers are "wa" and "ga." In the following example, "musuko" means "my son':

> English grammar: "My son is four years old."
> Japanese grammar: "My son four years is."
> Japanese: "Musuko wa yon sai desu."

Question Markers

Like "wa" and "ga", "ka" is a marker that doesn't have a direct word translation in English, but it changes the sentence. In this case, it changes a sentence into a question.

> English grammar: "What is it?"
> Japanese grammar: "What is?"
> Japanese: "Nan desu ka?"

Negation

The only verb conjugation you absolutely need to become familiar with is the use of a verb to imply positive or negative affirmation. The default is the positive variation, and is indicated by an ending of -masu. For example, "to eat" is "tabemasu." The negative variation, or "to not eat", changes the suffix of the verb to -masen. Thus, "tabemasen" means "don't eat."

> English grammar: "I eat tuna."
> Japanese grammar: "tuna eat."
> Japanese: "Tsuna tabemasu."

> English grammar: "I don't eat octopus."
> Japanese grammar: "octopus not-eat."
> Japanese: "Tako tabemasen."

Other Verb Suffixes

To change a verb to the past tense, change the –masu ending of the verb to –mashita.

> English grammar: "I come from Kyoto."
> Japanese grammar: "Kyoto from come."
> Japanese: "Kyoto kara kimasu."

> English grammar: "I came from Kyoto."
> Japanese grammar: "Kyoto from came."
> Japanese: "Kyoto kara kimashita."

To indicate "want to," change the –masu ending of the verb to –tai, and also use desu.

> English grammar: "I eat octopus."
> Japanese grammar: "octopus eat."
> Japanese: "Tako tabemasu."

> English grammar: "I want to eat octopus."
> Japanese grammar: "octopus eat-want be."
> Japanese: "Tako tabetai desu."

Phrases About Speaking Japanese

Ehgo hanasemasu ka? – Can you speak English?
Nihon go dekimasen – I don't speak Japanese
Mo ichido itte, onegai shimasu – Say it again, please
Yukkuri hanashite, onegai shimasu – Please speak slowly
Ehgo de nan desu ka? – What is it in English?
Zenzen hanasemasen – I can't speak at all
Zenzen dame desu - Completely bad
Sukoshi - A little

Numbers and Counting

There are multiple number systems in Japanese, which can be one of the most difficult concepts for English speakers to master. Yet with a little effort, these concepts can be kept separate. Just remember that the context determines which system to use.

The most basic numbering system is used for counting and for money. When you're shopping, an item's cost will be specified using this system.

1. Ichi
2. Ni
3. San
4. Yon (also Shi)
5. Go
6. Roku
7. Nana (also Shichi)
8. Hachi
9. Kyu
10. Juu

After reaching ten, numbers start over in a completely predictable pattern: eleven is juu-ichi, twelve is juu-ni, and so on up to nineteen, which is juu-kyu.

Twenty is simply "two-tens", or ni-juu. Twenty-one is ni-juu-ichi, and twenty-two is ni-juu-ni. This continues through ninety-nine (kyu-juu-kyu). Then the process starts over with hyaku (hundred), again at sen (thousand), and again at man (ten thousand). Here are some samples:

781: nana-hyaku hachi-juu-ichi

1965: sen kyu-hyaku roku-juu-go

The pronunciation differs for some numbers: 300 is sanbyaku, 600 is roppyaku, and 800 is happyaku.

The word for yen is pronounced "en", so you may hear a price like this: "ni-sen yon-hyaku san-juu-ichi en" (¥2,431).

The second number system is strictly for counting people. This system is only different for number 1 and number 2:

1. hitori
2. futari

For three and beyond, the previously-explained counting system is used. When talking about people, you would add "nin" to the number:

>Three people = san nin
>Four people = yon nin
>Etc.

Note that "nin" is not added to hitori or futari. The concept is built into the word.

The final number system is for quantities of items. You might use this system when requesting a certain number of items during shopping or dining (though not, however, for the cost, which uses the previously-explained counting system). The number system for quantities is not to be used to refer to living beings.

1. hitotsu
2. futatsu
3. mittsu
4. yottsu
5. itsutsu
6. muttsu
7. nanatsu
8. yattsu
9. kokonotsu
10. too

Phrases for Rides/Attractions

Nanmei (sama) desu ka? – How many?

Hitori – 1 person

Futari – 2 people

San–nin – 3 people

Yo–nin – 4 people

Bahn-go – row

Koutai joushya dekimasu ka? – Can we do child switch here?

Koutai riyou kaado... arismasu ka? – Do you have a child-switch card?

Sumimasen ga, ichiban mae onegai shimasu – Excuse me, front row please.

Dono kurai machinmasu ka? – How long is the wait?

Pareedo wa nanji kara desu ka? – What time will the parade start?

Hanabi wa nanji kara desu ka? – What time will the parade start?

Hanabi was koko de miremasu ka? – Can I watch the fireworks from here?

Mickey was doko de aemasuka? – Where can I meet Mickey?

Phrases for Dining

Ehgo no menyuu wa arimasu ka? – Do you have an English menu?

Ookii – large (as in a soda size)

Kore desu – this one

Toe – "and" (in the midst of ordering)

Mata – also

Set-oh – combo meal (the "set")

Tabemasu – to eat

Tabemasen – not eat

Tabetai desu – want to eat

Nomimasu – to drink

Nomitai desu – want to drink

Kin'en seki – non smoking

Onaka ippai – I'm full

Kore wa nan desu ka? – What is this?

Kore kudasai – I'll take this, please

Osusame wa? – What do you recommend?

Omizu kudasai – May I have water, please

Do desu ka? – how is it?

ii desu – good

Suki desu – I like this (ski des)

Oishikatta desu – It was delicious

Chotto – (I only like it) a little

Mama deshita – it was so so

Shokuji – dinner or meal

Phrases for Shopping

_____ Arimasu ka? Do you have ___?

Sore wa ikura desu ka? – how much is it?

Kore – this (close to me)

Sore – that (close to you)

Are – that (close to nobody)

Ookii – big

Chiisai – small

Kore da ke desu – this is all (I'm ready to check out)

Phrases About You

Amerika no Florida kara kimashita – I come from (America's) Florida

Kyoshi desu – I am a teacher

Yochien–ji desu – preschool student

Nan–sai desu ka? – how many years old are you?

O–ikutsu desu ka? – how old are you?

Watashi wa 37–sai desu – I am 37 years old

ototo san – little brother
onii san – older brother
imouto – little sister
one san – older sister
aka–chan – baby
otou-san – father
okaa-san - mother
kodomo – my children
musume – my daughter
musuko – my son
musuko wa yon sai desu – my son is 4 years old
tomodachi - friend

Bathroom
Toire wa doko desu ka? – where is the bathroom?

Travel and Directions
Kyoto ni ikimasu – to go to Kyoto
Shinkansen de kimashita – came by shinakansen (bullet train)
Eki - station

Shinkansen no Eki – train station

Maihama Eki wa doku desu ka? Where is Maihama station?

Kippu uriba – ticket machine

Tokyo made ikura desu ka? – how much to Tokyo?

Hoteru – hotel

Basu–tei – bus stop

Koko / soko / asoko – here, there, over there

Mighini – right

Hidari – left

Ushiro ni arimasu – behind

Mae ni arimasu – front

Yoko ni arimasu – next to

Massugu – straight

Ue ni agarimasu – go up

Shita ni orimasu – go down

Ichi–kai ni arimus – on the first floor

Takushii noriba – taxi stand

MiraCosta hoteru ni onegai shimasu – To the MiraCosta hotel
    please

Ikkai – first floor

Rokkai – sixth floor

Hakkai – eighth floor

Time and Calendar

Go hun – 5 minutes

Juppun – 10 minutes

San juppun – 30 minutes

Ichi jikan – 1 hour

Ni–ji go–fun – 2:05 (two hour, five minute)

Gozen – am / gogo – pm

Gatsu = month (May = go-gatsu, June = roku–gatsu)

Nichiyobi – Sunday

Getsuyobi – Monday

Kayobi – Tuesday

Suiyobi – Wednesday
Mokuyobi – Thursday
Kinyobi – Friday
Doyobi – Saturday
Dono kurai (nan nichi) nihon ni imasu ka? – How long (how
    many days) are you staying in Japan?
Ishyuukan desu – 1 week
Touka kan desu – 10 days
Ashita – tomorrow
Kinou – yesterday
Asa – morning
Hiru – noon
Yoru – night

Colors

Aka – red
Ao – blue
Kiiro – yellow
Midori – green
Kuro – black
Shiro – white
Orenji – orange
Gure – gray
Chairo – brown

Other General Words

Moe – also
Toe – and
Totemo – very
ii desu ne – sounds good (nice) / looks good / seems fine
so desu ne – yeah, right? / yes, I think so / yes, I agree / that's
right, isn't it? / Let's see.
Itsu – when

Nan–ji – what time
Doshite – why
Ikimasu – to go
(suffix –tai) – want
Disneyland ni ikitai
    desu – I want to
    go to Disneyland
Kimasu – to come
Kimashita – came

Shimasu – to do (simply add it to nouns: "denwa o shimasu"
    means to do/make a phone call)
Arimasu – to be (sometimes used as though it means "to
    have")

Venturing Outside Disney

Choosing Hotels and Having a "Home Base" Hotel

If you decide to explore Japan beyond Disney, which is a great idea (you've come this far, why not set aside a few extra days?) then you'll have to do some extra planning on where to stay. Consult a guide book to Japan for ideas on which cities to visit, and how much time to spend at each place. Once you know the cities and dates, go online to book a hotel.

If you'd like to approximate the usual Western hotel experience as much as possible, stick with names you already know. On hotels.com, you can find information about Comfort Inn, Best Western, and many hotel chains that will be quite familiar. The experience inside their Japanese outlets will also be familiar. You can expect their staff members to speak a reasonable amount of English.

One aspect you may wish to consider is where the hotel is located. Since you're probably not traveling by car, you'll be arriving via train. It's usually worthwhile to pay a higher price for a hotel room just to be within walking distance of the train station. Conversely, if adventure is your calling, you can always take a taxi or use public transportation, such as subways or trolley-like streetcars.

As noted above, hotels.com has a good sampling of chains whose names will be familiar. But for price, it's hard to beat Rakuten Travel (http://travel.rakuten.co.jp/en). Searching its database for hotels yields some of the same results as hotels.com, but also many additional options. If you visit one of these hotels, your experience will be more authentically

Japanese. Depending on your degree of flexibility, you may wish to sample a Ryokan (Japanese style) room, which is laid out totally differently. Expect only a low table and bare bamboo floors, which will later become a communal sleeping area, courtesy of mats and blankets which are stored in the wall closets.

Traveling around Japan means using the bullet trains, which do not offer any particular luggage storage. If the trains are crowded, you do not want to be stuck dragging around either large suitcases or a bunch of smaller bags. There's a better option: begin and end your vacation in Japan at the Tokyo Disney Resort. Spend at least one night in a hotel there on each leg of your visit. Bookending your travel around the country this way gives you a "home base" hotel at Tokyo Disney. The primary advantage is that you can leave the majority of your bags at your home base hotel while you are traveling on the bullet trains, allowing you to travel lightly.

As an alternative to a home base hotel, you can ask your first hotel to have your luggage forwarded, if you're staying at the same hotel chain in the next city. This usually costs very little.

Japan Rail Pass

For about the price of one round-trip ticket to Kyoto, international visitors can opt to buy a seven-day unlimited pass for the bullet trains and then travel around the country quickly and relatively cheaply. The Japan Rail Pass (JR Pass) must be purchased at an authorized travel agency before your trip begins—you cannot buy it in Japan. If your local agent doesn't provide this service, consider I-ACE travel, which specializes in trips to Japan (http://www.iace-usa.com).

Children under six will not need tickets, the assumption being that they can sit on your lap if necessary. If there are empty seats, feel free to spread out and place your children on them. This is especially common in the "green" cars, which are the first-class carriages on the bullet trains. If you have more than two children aged 1-5, the additional children be charged a youth fare.

You definitely will want to pay the surcharge for Green cars when you buy the JR Pass. It's not much of an additional cost and you'll enjoy greater comfort, much more space, and far fewer travelers sharing space with you.

The primary bullet trains in Japan are known as Shinkansen. Your JR Pass will work on all of them, as well as the local JR trains within cities. The only trains they won't work on are called Nozomi, which travel the same stretches as the Shinkansen but make fewer stops and travel just a little bit faster. Don't worry that you won't be on the very fastest of the bullet trains—the surcharge isn't worth the minimal time savings.

Note: be careful that you don't accidentally purchase a "JR East Pass," which admittedly sounds a lot like a regular JR Pass. The JR East Pass gets you out of the eastern part of the country (Kyoto and beyond, for instance, are not included).

With the JR Pass, you can make seat reservations for individual trains, though this isn't absolutely required. Still, it's a good idea. See below for more information.

Most Shinkansen trains don't have a dining car, but there are restrooms on each car. A concessions cart will come rolling through your car after every stop.

You'll have to show your JR Pass to gain access to the Shinkansen portion of the train station. These bullet trains only stop once per city, and not in every city at that. In the city of Tokyo, the main train station is also called Tokyo on the maps and subway routes. To take a Shinkansen, you have to make your way to the Tokyo Station, then show your JR Pass again to access the Shinkansen sub-station.

You won't be asked about tickets again until you are aboard and under way. If you have seat reservations, simply show your seat reservation tickets. Otherwise, showing your JR Pass will suffice. You won't be asked to show your tickets again on this journey, though the conductor will pass through after each stop to check the tickets of anyone who recently boarded.

If you do have a JR Pass, you can use it on all of the JR trains in Tokyo, meaning you can avoid the separate subway system entirely. JR Passes have to be purchased for seven or fourteen consecutive days of use. You may wish to plan your visit so that you activate the pass while traveling around Tokyo, then continue using it to travel about the country.

You must bring your JR Pass voucher with you when you come to Japan, but this voucher isn't a valid pass until activated. Unfortunately, there is no office to do that at Maihama station at the Tokyo Disney Resort. You'll want to activate it either when you land at the airport, or by traveling back to Tokyo Station and then activating it at the JR East Office. Once you activate it, the seven-day countdown begins. Don't activate it until you plan to start traveling!

If you want to visit Tokyo Disney first and travel the country later, just use the bus to get to your hotel. On the day you wish to travel the country, make your way to the Maihama JR station, carrying your JR Pass voucher with you. Keep it hidden for the time being. You need to buy a one-way ticket to Tokyo Station in the "usual" fashion first. This can be done with the assistance of the live person to the left of the gates, or via the automated machines to the right of the gates. The touch screen machines let you switch to English, and from there you can navigate easily. The machine will accept your cash and issue you a ticket directly. Take this to the gates and insert it. The ticket will pop back up at the top as the gate opens. Take the ticket with you, as you'll need it to get out of the station when you reach your destination.

Head upstairs and wait on the side of the platform heading to Tokyo. This will be the side closest to the Tokyo Disney Resort. If you get on a train on the other side, you'll be heading the wrong way! If that happens, don't panic. Just get off at the next station, cross the platform, and wait for the correct train to arrive—it costs nothing extra.

When you arrive at Tokyo Station, use your ticket to pass through the gates at the Yaesu North Exit. This time, the ticket will not pop out again. Just walk through. Find the JR East office, activate your pass, and, for the next seven days, you won't need to purchase any train tickets. (Note: your entire party will need to come with you on this pass-activation journey. The passports will have to be presented and photocopied to transform vouchers into valid JR Passes.)

Navigating Train Stations

Trains in Japan are first organized into "lines" (the Keiyo line, for instance, is the one that will stop at Maihama station) and then into "directions'. Generally speaking, the last station of the line determines how a train is labeled. For instance, the trains on the Keiyo line may be headed toward Tokyo or Soga. Find your own position on the station map to know which train you'll want to take in order to arrive at your destination. If you're at Shin-Kiba and wish to travel to Maihama, it won't work to take the Keiyo line toward Tokyo Station. You will need to take the Keiyo line toward Soga.

Things get a touch more complicated when there are trains that go in the same direction, but which may not go all the way to the last station in the line. In that event, the train will be labeled with the last station it visits. Thus, there are trains on the Keiyo line headed to the terminus at Kisarazu, and others that terminate when they get to Soga, which is one of the stops on the way. If your destination is on the way for either train, you can hop on any one headed in the right direction. The same holds true for lines that split at the end and proceed toward different terminal stations.

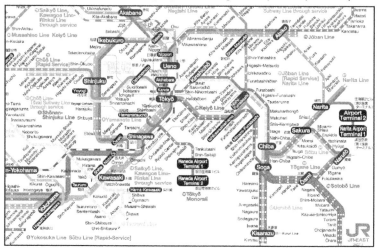

As you make your way through train stations, watch first for the names of the train lines, which are posted on signs hanging from the ceiling. Often, these are color-coded as well (for instance, the Keiyo line at Tokyo Station is always indicated with a red sign). These signs will guide you to the right platform. Then you just have to decide which side of the platform to be on, based on the direction you want to go.

Usually there are signs specific to each side of the platform, indicating which stops will be made by a train going in that direction.

Once you get on a train, stay alert for the first station. You should have a printed map of the stations, since schematics of the route may be visible inside the car (especially above the doors), but only in Japanese. Identify which station is coming up next, assuming the train is moving in the right direction. Then, as the train pulls in to the next station, look out the windows every so often to find the station name on signs. This will help you verify that the train is going in the correct direction (or clue you in that it's not, in which case you should disembark and switch platform sides).

As the train slows down, start looking for the station name. You might get lucky and have the train stop so that the station name is visible from your window, but since the signs aren't that common, you might not be so fortunate. In that event, you won't know when you've reached your destination. Start watching early.

There's one last complication. Some trains are considered "rapid" and skip some of the stops posted on the map. The train will be labeled "rapid" (in English) on the front, so watch for that word. A map on the platform will explain which stops the rapid train does make. It could be that the stop you want is still made by the rapid train, in which case you merely need to pay attention and not miss it. Otherwise, you'll want to wait for the next train after the rapid train.

Other signs on the platform might explain how long the trains are, and where exactly on the platform they stop, so you will know where to line up for them. In slower periods, lining up isn't necessary, but this is hardly the case all of the time.

Bullet trains work a bit differently from normal JR trains. First, they make stops in a "station within a station," so you will have to gain access to the Shinkansen zone of a station to find the right platforms. Second, the lines bear names unrelated to the destinations. For instance, the Tokyo-Kyoto trip might take place on Hikari 373 (or perhaps the Hikari 413, or several other possible variations). The Shinkansen trains have names corresponding with their types, such as Hikari or Kodama. Since there are multiple Hikari trains, numbers are used to specify exactly which Hikari train is traveling on a given stretch. Thus, it may be that Hikari 375 is going from Tokyo to Kyoto at 13:36, while Hikari 415 is traveling the same stretch at 14:06, half an hour later.

Bullet Train Reservations

There's no need (or way) to make train reservations before arriving in Japan. You must, however, research your desired destinations and timetables before your vacation begins. It is best to print out your exact requests and bring the information with you. This makes the reservations process a snap; just hand the entire sheet to the reservations agent. It might look like this:

Japan Rail Pass - Green Car Reservations

October 15
SHINKANSEN HIKARI 405
Depart Tokyo 9:06
Arrive Kyoto 11:43

October 16
SHINKANSEN HIKARI 377
Depart Kyoto 17:21
Arrive Shinosaka 17:36

SHINKANSEN HIKARI RailStar 479
Depart Shinosaka 17:59
Arrive Hiroshima 19:28

October 17
SHINKANSEN HIKARI RailStar 468
Depart Hiroshima 16:10
Arrive Shinosaka 17:44

SHINKANSEN HIKARI 424
Depart Shinosaka 18:19
Arrive Tokyo 21:13

You may find the timetables on the official website, http://www.jreast.co.jp/e/, to be daunting. The most convenient site on which to view timetables online is http://www.hyperdia.com, where you have greater control over variables, including the ability to specify a Green car, and to exclude Nozomi (which is not included with a JR Pass, anyway).

When you make reservations, you should be aware that there is such a thing as a "quiet car", where noise of any kind, including talking, is discouraged. Travelers with children should avoid this option. Others may wish to seek it out.

Trains leave punctually. If you are late, you may not make it onto the train for which you have reservations. Don't fret. Simply head to the JR office in that station (if the city is big enough to have a Shinkansen stop, it will be big enough to have a JR office), and quietly explain, in English, that you have missed your train and need a new reservation. It may expedite matters if you hand over the reservations you no longer need, since that will show your destination and route. The attendant should be able to quickly come up with another option for you. Unless it's the end of the day, odds are good that your delay will last less than an hour.

City Maps

Good guidebooks about Japan include rudimentary street maps of the larger cities. You may also wish to visit the tourist information counters found at airports and train stations in the larger cities. There you can obtain free street maps.

Toilet Topics

Restrooms at the Tokyo Disney Resort and the associated hotels will contain just about everything you would expect. Be sure to sample the high-powered hand dryers; just insert your hands limply into the slot and warm air will come at them from both sides.

Outside the Tokyo Disney Resort, though, things are quite different. Most noticeably, you won't find hand towels or air dryers, so it's important to bring either handkerchiefs or pocket tissues. Otherwise, you're down to either wiping your hands on your pants or just letting them air-dry.

Odds are good that you won't find soap in these bathrooms, either. An essential item to bring from home is a small bottle of alcohol-based hand sanitizer.

Another surprise may be awaiting you inside the stalls. In most facilities, and especially in older facilities, you may only find one stall (or even none!) with the familiar style of toilet, called "Western-style" in Japan. Instead, you will find Japanese-style toilets, which are very low-to-the-ground minimalist porcelain pits.

These are meant to be used while squatting and facing the raised lip. It is not uncommon for the ground near the toilet to be somewhat unsanitary. As a result, even the Japanese prefer the Western-style toilet. You may find people lining up for the Western-style stalls while leaving the Japanese-style stalls vacant.

Western visitors to the men's room are sometimes startled to discover female bathroom attendants cleaning the sinks and toilets without first asking all men to vacate the area.

There are bathrooms identified for handicapped use at subways, train stations, and some hotels. These are stand-alone rooms, not part of regular restrooms, and often have sliding glass doors that lock electronically. Diaper changing tables are often found in these handicapped-only bathrooms.

Japanese Signs and Asking Directions

All signs at the Tokyo Disney Resort are presented in both Japanese and English. This is true in well-traveled areas (like Tokyo Station) as well. However, the further off the beaten path you travel, the more likely it becomes that signs will be written only in Japanese. Some streets may have no street signs at all.

A good guidebook to Japan will include directions to your destination. It may be worthwhile to look up this information online prior to your vacation, print out the directions, and bring them along.

However, this will not help in every instance. Street signs will be in Japanese characters and thus unreadable for most Western visitors. To counteract this problem, locate a map at the train station, probably on a stanchion, that lists nearby

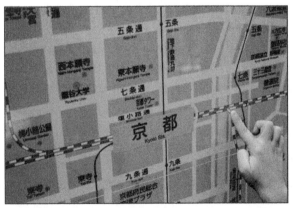

attractions. That map usually will feature street names in English, as well as those of prominent buildings and natural features. Snap a digital photo of this map. You can continue to reference it as you travel around the area.

Even the most seasoned and prepared travelers sometimes find it necessary to ask for directions. You will find residents to be extremely polite and helpful, though gesticulation, pointing at the map, and half-phrases may be more common than complete sentences. You may even be escorted personally to your destination by a stranger! In fact, if you open up a map and appear lost, a helpful resident may approach you before you think to ask for assistance.

Miscellaneous Customs

Politeness toward strangers does not apply to every circumstance. The elderly and disabled receive priority access. They may simply walk to the front of any line without saying a word and not think twice about stepping in ahead of you.

Also, the respect for personal space which is evident on the parade route at Tokyo Disney Resort is not on display when it comes to public transportation. Expect elevators to be crowded beyond the normal Western standards. The same holds true for subways and trains, especially during busy commuting hours.

Cars travel on the left side of the street; however, pedestrian traffic works the opposite way. Walk on the right side of a sidewalk. Similarly, on escalators and moving sidewalks, the right side is reserved for people who are walking. If you wish to stand, stand to the left side. This is the opposite of the custom in the United States.

Perhaps because conditions are sometimes crowded, respect for personal hygiene is universal. That includes consideration of others when sick. You will undoubtedly encounter people wearing gauze masks over their nose and mouth. This is done as a courtesy to everyone else, so that coughing will not infect anyone else. People generally do not blow their noses in public. It's considered rude, and many opt to sneeze directly at the ground, rather than make their hands dirty by covering their mouth and nose. If they have a tissue, they may dab gently at their nose.

Cleanliness does not extend to the air, though, when it comes to smoking. Expect to find that most eateries have both smoking and non-smoking sections, but with the two zones divided by nothing at all, effectively rendering the entire atmosphere a smoking area.

You'll see a lot of wrappers within boxes within wrappers within bags—the wasteful packaging extends to the extra bags received when you buy gifts at Tokyo Disney Resort shops—and you may not see a lot of paper and cardboard recycling. Some trash sorting is encouraged by specialized bins in train stations. Plastic bottles are recycled religiously, particularly those labeled "PET" on the side.

Last, a word about bowing. You may see slight bows in dining and shopping interactions, but deep bows are usually reserved for meeting new people professionally, which most tourists don't do. The Japanese themselves often do not bow when interacting with someone in a customer service relationship, so you won't need to, either. On top of this, you are probably not expected, as a foreigner, to understand how and when to bow. No offense will be taken if you fail to do so. You are safest merely observing the ritual and not trying to imitate it.

Returning Home

Checking Out of the Hotel

Contrary to most Western hotels, some hotels in Japan ask you to sign your credit card draft when you first check in, so there is no need to sign again on your way out. You may, however, be asked whether you used the mini bar or stocked refrigerator on your last night.

It may feel anticlimactic, but that's all there is. Sometimes a receipt is produced, but often it is not. If you need to store luggage for later in the day, or even for several days, visit the bell desk to make your inquiry. (They also speak excellent English.) When your luggage is taken, you'll be issued a receipt, which you must guard carefully. You'll need it to get your stuff back later!

Transferring to Narita Airport

You have the same options open for your return that were available for your arrival: taxi, train, and bus. If you have a valid JR Pass, you can use it to return to the airport. Or tell the attendant at the window that you want a ticket to Narita airport.

Just travel on local JR trains to Tokyo Station and switch to the Narita Airport line (follow the blue signs). Just be aware that from Maihama some of the trains terminate before they make it to Tokyo Station (one example is the Kaihimmakuhari train). Your JR Pass will also work on the Narita Express (NEX) train.

The simpler option is to use the shuttle bus, Friendly Airport Limousine. You can buy tickets for this bus right at your hotel if you're staying at either a Disney hotel or an official hotel. You can buy these tickets "same day", but you won't be able to buy them from the bus driver directly. Ask at the hotel's front desk where they are available. You can use either a credit card or cash to buy the ticket.

Assume that the journey will last 80 minutes (though it could be little as 45), and that the bus will probably stop at multiple hotels for additional passengers, creating additional delays. Make sure you leave early enough to make your flight! The schedule is often posted at the hotel where the bus will pick you up.

The bus will make multiple stops at Narita Airport. Depending on who is riding in the bus with you, your stop may be as late as the third stop. (If there are only international travelers, it may be the first stop.) You will hear announcements in the bus in both Japanese and English regarding which stop is next. Listen carefully, as the announcements may not be very loud.

Check-In at the Airline

When you leave the bus, walk through the doors of the terminal and locate your airline. Before you reach the ticket and check-in stations, you'll enter into a semi-secure zone. There are no metal detectors here, but all bags and carry-on luggage will have to pass through an X-ray machine. The bags will be marked as they are inspected. If you need to make any adjustments, such as transfer objects from your carry-on bags to your checked luggage, do so before you come to the X-ray machine.

You can then proceed to a kiosk to check in with a live person. You'll be asked to pass your luggage forward to be checked in, which should bear the stickers of the X-ray machine you just passed through. You won't see this luggage again until you arrive at your international destination.

After obtaining your boarding passes, you leave the semi-secure zone and head back out to the main airport. There is a somewhat large shopping mall in this part of the Narita airport, with quite a variety of gift ideas for relatives back home, and prices that are not too exorbitant. Finish this shopping (or eating; there's a good and inexpensive food court here too) before you head toward the gates.

To access the departure gates, you have to pass through the usual security checks. This time around you will pass through a metal detector, as your carry-on items are put through an x-ray test. The same restrictions apply here as in the United States: no liquids, gels, creams, or potentially lethal artifacts. In Japan, you may be fined if these are found in your possession.

After the security checks, you'll proceed through customs on the way out. You'll need your boarding passes and passports handy for this. Normally, you won't be asked anything at this stage, and you should be on your way after your papers are subjected to a cursory examination.

Returning Home and Recovering
The flight back may be shorter than your flight to Japan. If you're traveling to the United States, on this leg you'll have the jet stream at your back. The journey may be shorter by an hour or more.

You'll be handed a customs form on the plane, one per family. Expect to pass through customs upon your return in a similar process to the one you encountered in Japan.

Expect significant jet lag during the ensuing week. Even some experienced travelers report sleep pattern disruptions, despite their best efforts to stay awake longer (or sleep earlier) on the first day to adjust more quickly. Somehow, it still takes several days to adjust. A sleeping pill on the first night may help to "reset" your body.

Last, there may be some surprises on your credit card bills, such as conversion fees for every purchase (this is not the case for all credit and debit cards). One of the more unusual surprises is that you may see no mention of overseas purchases on your next credit card bill. This is not a windfall! The credit card issuers are sometimes just slow in adding foreign charges to your account. Rest assured that those charges will show up eventually! In the meantime, you may want to be cautious of your credit limit. The charges may pop into existence all at once.

Planning Your Next Visit

The greatest shock, financially speaking, may be the tendency of tourists returning from the Tokyo Disney Resort to instantly plan a return trip. The magic of these parks inevitably infects every visitor. While you may bask in the glow of your first visit for some time, the desire to return can be overwhelming. The Tokyo Disney parks are unique in the world. The urge to visit them frequently will be overpowering for some people. I suggest you not resist the "yen." Would it be so bad to become a seasoned and experienced traveler to Tokyo Disneyland and Tokyo DisneySea?

About the Author

Kevin Yee is a Central Florida-based writer who has written weekly articles about Disney theme parks for numerous websites since 1996. His fascination with the parks began during his 15-year career working for Disneyland in the 80s and 90s.

He is the author of the popular *Walt Disney World Hidden History* book, which highlights remnants of former attractions still found at the parks, reveals the intentional tributes to old rides and to the Imagineers that build them, and catalogs the inside jokes that hide in plain sight.

Since 2010, Kevin has published an annual *Walt Disney World 'Earbook*, mostly because he thought it would be a neat idea to always have a way to travel back in time using books, the way we use high school yearbooks. And really, isn't Walt Disney World just like an old friend you see every so often?

He has also written extensively about other Disney theme parks. His works, some which were created with co-authors, include *Epcot—The First Thirty Years*, *Top Tips for Visiting Disneyland Paris*, *Mouse Trap—Memoir of a Disneyland Cast Member*, *Jason's Disneyland Almanac* (a daily history of the Anaheim parks), *101 Things You Never Knew About Disneyland*, and *Magic Quizdom*, a Disneyland trivia book.

Made in the USA
Las Vegas, NV
18 July 2024